POWER SPEAKING
THAT GETS RESULTS

By the Same Author

Run-And-Shoot Football: Offense of the Future

POWER SPEAKING THAT GETS RESULTS

Glenn "Tiger" Ellison

Parker Publishing Company, Inc.
West Nyack, New York

Dedication

To Atchi
Of the bubbling spirit
Whose tireless footsteps
And guiding light
And little no-no's
Led this humble mortal
To a better
More thrilling
Life

© 1974, by

PARKER PUBLISHING COMPANY, INC.

West Nyack, N.Y.

Library of Congress Cataloging in Publication Data

Ellison, Glenn.
    Power speaking that gets results.

    1. Public speaking. I. Title.
PN4121.E464   1974   808.5'1   73-19983
ISBN 0-13-687004-X

Printed in the United States of America

YOUR MAGIC FORMULA FOR POWER

When you were four years old you could shuffle your tiny torso out upon a parlor rug and face a roomful of admiring people without a quaver in your bubbling heart. You could open your small mouth and pour out words in tones that were crystal clear. Your gestures flowed with your words, spontaneous and natural. You communicated.

Can you do it now? As a tiny tot you were a regular little Power Speaker. Have you changed? With your bigger body and greater strength can you still speak with persuasive power? Can you hold the attention of your boss and your fellow workers and your customers and your wife and your kids? Do you know how to win that trip to Hawaii and that raise in salary and a membership in the Noble Knights of Power Speaking?

Anybody can do these things but most people don't because 90 percent of all people everywhere neglect the God-given talent that is so vital to success and happiness. Sleepy-eyed people the wide world over go cruising around sniffing for some magic formula that will open the way to a good, thrilling life.

How absolutely amazing! Right there beneath their very noses, floating to-and-fro in clear, vivid view of all with eyes to see, *is the magic formula!* The formula is so simple yet so vital to human welfare that the astounding puzzle of modern times is that only 10 percent of the world's population take advantage of it.

Reading this book makes you my client. I want to do some things for you, Mr. Client. I want to give you a vivid look at a formula for success that refuses to fail. I want to paint you a clear picture of tiny men growing to greatness because they developed one basic skill and used one natural talent. I want to turn your gaze upon strong men tottering toward failure because they misused this God-given talent. I want to convince you that as a normal human being you can become a heroic animal capable of leading your fellowman to a good, thrilling life. I want to show you a wide open road that will lead you and yours to greater security, wider recognition, and a world of romance.

Speech is the God-given talent. *Power* is the man-made way. *Power speech* is the man-made way of using your God-given talent. Whether you send your spoken words down from a podium or across a dinner table or over the boss's desk, the most effective way in all this world to communicate with your fellowman and to get him to go your way is *Power Speaking That Gets Results.*

This book will lay the whole process out before your eyes. The understanding will be easy. The reading will be fun.

"Go get 'em, Tiger!"

ACKNOWLEDGMENTS

Thanks to Elmo Lingrel who showed *power* on the field and to Wade Miller who demonstrated *power* in the school house and to Woody Hayes who spread *power* across the campus and to Rocko Joslin who spewed *power* during the ball game and to Mom and Dad who wielded *power* at the woodshed and to all those thousands of others who crammed my memory storehouse with *powerful* mental pictures to talk about and to write about.

CONTENTS

1

WORDS THAT EXPLODE

Once upon a time a lovely lady got up from her tall throne, stuck her cute little nose into the South East, and saw coming toward her the greatest flotilla of battleboats the world had ever known: *The mighty Spanish Armada was coming to destroy England!*

'Frobisher! Hawkins! Drake!'' cried Queen Elizabeth, "Give us leadership! Go forth, men. Stop the mighty Spanish Armada. Turn them around. Send them home. If you fail, fellows our goose is cooked, our duck is dead, our gosling is gone Frobisher! Hawkins! Drake! *Last call for leadership! Go!''*

They went. They stopped the mighty Spanish Armada. They knocked it cold! They killed it dead! They sank half those big battleboats and the other half crashed on the rock-bound coast of Scotland. Not one Spanish ship ever returned home to Spain—*not one single ship!*

"Frobisher, Hawkins, Drake," smiled Queen Elizabeth sweetly as she tapped each man on his head with his sword gently, making him a Knight of the Golden Garter, "from this day henceforth England will be master of the high seas, monarch of the waterways. Nobody can stop us. Three great ships in our navy will make us number one in this world. The name of the first ship? *Craftsmanship*—we'll build the finest ship afloat. The name of the second ship? *Seamanship*—we'll sail the finest ship afloat. The name of the third ship? *Leadership*—we'll captain the finest ship afloat. Craftsmanship, seamanship, leadership—these three—and the greatest of these is *leadership.*

THE MOST DYNAMIC FORCE EVER KNOWN

Now, Mr. Persuasive Speaker—I know you are a persuasive fellow or on your way to becoming one or else you would not be reading this book—the lovely lady Elizabeth was not just idly blowing the breeze, she knew exactly whereof she spoke: *The most dynamic force the world has known since time began is a thing called leadership.*

Now then, I want to give you a definition; I want you to think with me for two minutes. I know thinking is hard work. A fellow has to sweat to think. But give me a couple of minutes and then we'll loosen it up again.

Look—definition: *Leadership* is a force with a *purpose* that uses *persuasion* as a tool to build *morale* as the stuff that *explodes into action and gets things done,* and getting things done is the purpose—*leadership gets things done.*

Persuasion is the tool with which you paint in the mind of anybody you lead a clear, vivid picture of the thing you want him to fight for, and at the same time you automatically kindle in his heart an intense, burning desire to fight for that particular thing—that's *persuasion;* that's the tool with which you build *morale*.

STUFF THAT SPEWS AND SPARKLES

Morale is the stuff, the intangible stuff down deep inside the person being led that begins to spew out into every part of his body when you paint in his mind a clear, vivid picture of the thing you want him to fight for, and when you kindle in his heart an intense burning desire to fight for that particular thing—that's *morale;* that's the stuff that *explodes into action and gets things done*.

Here's how it works: Everybody has a brain. You have a brain, I have a brain—all God's chillun have brains and nobody's brain is any bigger than anybody else's. Everybody's total brain weighs three pounds, but the part you think with weighs *only five ounces*. You have a little five-ounce thinking brain, fellow, but so does everybody else. Only 10 percent of your total brain is your thinking-brain. Ninety percent of it is your feeling-brain. Your feelings are nine times as strong as your thoughts, and that's just the reason that 90 percent of the things you and I do we do, not because we think we ought to do those things, but because we *feel* like doing them: our feelings take charge, our feelings dominate, our feelings dictate our actions—90 percent of the time. And, Mr. Persuasive Speaker, therein lies the *secret of verbal persuasion*.

GETTING THE LISTENER HUNGRY FOR ACTION

Every time you stand up to speak, you become a leader. So before you get up, sweat a little: establish in your mind one good solid thought, the thought you wish to shoot into your listener, the thing you want him to fight for, the action you want him to get going at. Then with that thought established pour all the feeling you've got in your body upon that thought, swamp that thought with feeling, and the thought becomes ten times as strong as it was before. Thought equals one, feeling equals nine, and thought plus feeling equals ten—thought plus feeling equals ten times the thought without the feeling, and that, Mr. Persuasive Speaker, is the *secret of persuasion:* Paint in the mind of your listener a clear, vivid picture of the thing you want him to fight for. This thing is your thought and this thought is a living thing. It pulsates with the life you poured into it. Your listener can see it. You *thought it* but he *sees it* because you painted him a picture of it. There it is, clear and vivid on the television screen of his little thinking-brain.

Now take a look at this: *His feeling-brain can see it, too.* Remember, a feeling-brain can't think but it can *see* and it loves to watch television, and every feeling brain *has a hot line* that leads right straight to the emotions. So the very instant the feeling-brain of your listener sees that clear, vivid picture you painted on his mental view-graph, that feeling-brain sends a quick message down to the emotions saying, "Crank it up down there, gang! We got big action today! *Sock it to 'em! Knock 'em down! Hit!"* Instantly his adrenal glands located right back behind his kidneys begin to squirt a thing called adrenalin into his blood stream, a thing called *morale* begins to spew out into every part of his body, he catches fire and rears back in his seat and he is ready, *ready,* READY! Ready for what? Ready to start fighting for that clear, vivid picture you painted in his mind because his feeling brain has grabbed that picture and rammed it into his heart where it becomes an intense, burning desire to fight for that particular thing. You were a leader, the great persuader—*you persuaded a listener.* Look at him: he bristles with morale and he's hungry for action.

HELP ARRIVING FOR A WOE-BE-GONE WORLD

Think with me once more—definition: *Leadership* is a force with a *purpose* that uses *persuasion* as a tool to build *morale* as the stuff that *explodes into action and gets things done*, and getting things done is the purpose—leadership gets things done. *Persuasion is the Power.*

The one thing this poor old uptight ball of earth needs above all else is a thing called *leadership*, whose secret weapon is a thing called *persuasion*. Therein lies your *Power*, Mr. Persuader.

2

EYE-POPPING PHRASES
THAT THROB IN THE HEART

Up in Calhoun County we had a country preacher who understood the secret of persuasion as well as anybody I ever saw in my life. He was a big rawbone fellow with very little education, who raised cotton six days a week and preached on Sunday. We didn't pay him anything except the few dimes we put in the collection plate, but he didn't mind because he loved to preach, and we loved to listen. He turned us on from the pulpit and we turned him on from the pews.

One Sunday he told us the story of David and Goliath, how the youngster laid the big man low with a slingshot.

"Now look, people," said the preacher, smacking his fist into his palm, "it was not just that little rock that killed that big bloke—*it was the way that damn kid throwed it!*"

The preacher paused a moment to permit us to call back the picture. Then he continued.

"He hit Goliath *in the eye* with that rock. Then he jumped on top of the big galoot and loosened the guy's armor and rammed the man's own sword into his big throbbing heart! David *hit him in the eye and stuck him in the heart!*"

Mr. Power Speaker, it's not just those little words that persuade that big audience—it's the way you throw them: *You hit them in the eye and stick them in the heart!*

HITTING THEM IN THE EYE

Everything that you and I know came to us through our eyes, our ears, our noses, our mouths, and our sense of touch. We know nothing that was not first clear and vivid in our five sense organs, and every single bit of every last thing we know is stored away in the art gallery of our feeling-brains in the form of a picture—millions of pictures, pretty pictures, ugly pictures, pictures big, pictures small, nice ones, naughty ones, all of them having come to us so clearly and vividly that they got themselves snatched up by our feeling-brains and rushed off below the border of our consciousness and recorded for future reference.

Fuzzy sensations go glimmering by without making an impression. The clear, vivid things are what we know and all we know. The sound of a sultry feminine voice floating in over your car radio in the quiet hours of the night brings to the television screen of your thinking-brain the willowy figure of the luscious creature who first got to you with that sound. You *listen* but you *see*—and you *feel*.

The sweet smell of lilacs brings back gently to your mental screen the lovely form of the little darling whose perfume smelled that way the night of the Junior Prom. You *smell* but you *see*—and you *feel*.

Whether you see a vivid thing or hear it or smell it or taste it or touch it, your feeling-brain comes bounding up and hustles the sensation off below the surface and records it as a picture.

You cannot to save your life avoid clear, vivid impressions. Each of them has to be recorded—as a *picture*. Let some big-bosomed blonde plop her delightful self down across from you at a banquet table as you listen to your wife's orders not to look, and you will *look* and you will *see* and you will *feel* and the picture will be recorded forevermore in the art gallery of your feeling-brain.

Slap somebody in the face with a skunk and dare him not to smell it—and he will smell it all right, and every time thereafter when he gets a good whiff of a skunk, he will see your ornery face.

Everything you and I know is recorded as a picture below the surface of our awareness. These pictures come popping back one by one as we experience sights and sounds and aromas in the world about us that call up those pictures. Glue sniffers and pot smokers and dope users stir up their feeling-brains so that a whole flurry of pictures storms their mental screens all at once. They call it "becoming aware." I call it "a bloomin' buzzin', mixed up confusion." They are aware not of the present but of the past, which comes pouring upon their mental screens in a garbled, distorted, furious mess. No wonder that occasionally one of them goes hurtling through a closed window and bounces his head on the sidewalk a few floors below—he had to bash the bats out of his belfry.

Eighty-five percent of your knowledge and mine came through our eyes and only 10 percent through our ears. The nerves that lead from the eye to the brain are twenty-five times as large as those from the ear to the brain. The Chinese proverb says it this way: "One time seeing is worth a thousand times hearing." Only 5 percent of what we know came through the nose, mouth, and sense of touch. Ninety-five percent of all our knowledge comes because we look and listen and learn. *Look, listen, learn*—that is 95 percent of all we'll ever know.

Mr. Persuasive Speaker, there's only one way in the whole wide world to get that audience to look and listen and learn: first you hit them in the *eye* with your words and then you stick them in the *heart* with a cause.

STICKING THEM IN THE HEART

Napoleon was only five feet two inches tall and he probably couldn't fight his way out of a strong paper sack, yet he was on his way to becoming the greatest leader of the Nineteenth Century. Do you know his secret? He knew how to *hit them in the eye and stick them in the heart*.

Said Napoleon when he was only twenty-five years old, "Look at those hollow bellies—you men are starving to death! Look at those uniforms on your backs—you're dressed in rags! Look at those barracks you're living in—nothing but shacks!

"Now listen, men, to me: I'll take you to a land that drips with milk and honey, where the streets are paved with gold, where there's food, clothing, and shelter in abundance for everybody. Come with me to Italy."

They went to Italy. It was an operation called *survival,* the greatest cause for action that burns in the human heart, *Operation Survival*.

When they had come and seen and conquered the land of the Romans, Napoleon said, "Look, men, at the wondrous deeds you have done in a few short years. Now hear this: come home with me to France, where our people will greet us at the border with wide-open arms saying, 'Hail to thee, National Champion, forevermore.'

"Come, men, home with me to France!"

They went home. It was an operation called *recognition,*

the second greatest cause for action that burns in the human heart, *Operation Recognition.*

Then said Napoleon, "We'll throw a party and invite pretty girls and eat good food and drink bubbly champagne and enjoy life."

They ate. They drank. They made merry. It was an operation called *romance,* the third greatest cause for action that burns in the human heart, *Operation Romance.*

Survival, recognition, romance—these three—and Napoleon was on his way to becoming the greatest leader of the Nineteenth Century. Why? Because he hit them in the *eye* with his words and he stuck them in the *heart* with a cause—until England hit him in the belly with a secret weapon called Wellington.

PUNCHING A RABBLE ROUSER IN THE BELLY

Adolph Hitler was only five feet five inches tall. I doubt whether he could lick anybody with his hands. Yet he was on his way to becoming the greatest leader of Twentieth Century Europe. His secret? He knew how *to hit them in the eye and stick them in the heart.*

Said Hitler: "Look at those blue eyes. Look at that fair hair. You men are the blue-eyed, fair-haired German Aryan. You were born to rule the world! Look at those black-eyed, shadow-skinned Jews. They have our money. We'll kill the Jew. We'll take the money. We'll put clothes on your back and food in your mouth and a gun in your hand. We'll fight for our rightful place in the world!"

This was Operation Survival.

"Then we'll move on Paris and knock out France. Then we'll move on London and knock out England. Then we'll move on Moscow and knock out Russia. Then we'll be the greatest country in Europe. After that we'll stand by ready to take on all comers. One day we'll be the greatest country in the world.''

This was Operation Recognition.

"Now and then we'll rest awhile and enjoy life: we'll eat good food and wear good clothes and sleep in good beds and procreate the Master Race.''

This was Operation Romance.

Survival, recognition, romance—these three—and Hitler was on his way to becoming the greatest leader of Twentieth Century Europe. Why? Because he not only knew how to hit people in the *eye* with his words but he also knew how to stick them in the *heart* with a cause—until England hit him in the belly with a secret weapon called Churchill.

COMING OF THE GREAT PERSUADER

Winston Churchill was only five feet seven inches tall. He was seventy years old. You wouldn't think he could whip anybody. Yet he stood with his feet planted and his black hat pulled down hard on his head, and he shook his fist at 2,000 German bombers that came over night after night dropping great doses of devastation upon England until England was on fire, England was burning up, England was going down to defeat for the first time since William the Conqueror stormed this rock in the channel back in 1066.

Said Churchill to his bewildered countrymen:

"We'll fight 'em on the oceanways, we'll fight 'em at the seashore, we'll fight 'em in the city streets, we'll fight 'em in the air, we'll fight 'em, fight 'em, fight 'em wherever they come at us.

'There'll always be an England
And England shall be free,

If England means as much to you
As England means to me.*' "

And England fought on and on and Winston Churchill became the greatest leader of the Twentieth Century. Why? Because he not only knew how to hit them in the *eye* with his words but he also knew how to stick them in the *heart* with a cause—so Winston Churchill goes striding into the history book as the Great Persuader of the Twentieth Century. When comes there a greater?

WONDERFUL WAY AND SO SIMPLE

How, Mr. Persuasive Speaker, does a person hit his listeners in the eye with his words, and how does he stick them in the heart with a cause? It is wonderfully easy and amazingly simple. Let's pin it down in the next chapter.

---

* Reprinted by permission of Gordon V. Thompson, Ltd., Toronto, Canada on behalf of Dash Music Company, Ltd., London, England.

3

THE WAY THAT SENTENCES
JUMP INTO ACTION

The very moment you have said hello to your audience you start painting a picture with your words. That picture gets their attention.

Do it like this:

Look at this hill here. The top of it is covered with the army of the Israelites just waiting here in the sunshine. Now look at that other hill over there. The top of it is covered with the army of the Philistines just waiting over there in the sunshine. Look at this valley in between with the shallow brook bubbling down the middle in the sunshine.

Every soul in the audience who has ever seen a hill or a valley or a brook or the light of the sun can see your picture in his mind's eye. He fills in your picture with his own hills and valleys and brooks, the ones that have impressed him over the years. And he *looks—but he won't look long* unless you do something with that picture: *make it move!*

Movement arouses curiosity. The listener wants to see what's happening. He's got to see where this thing is going. Show him:

> Down from the camp of the Philistines came Goliath, ten feet tall, dressed in armor from head to foot, nothing showing except his two big eyes and his big ugly face. In his right hand he swung a thirty-pound sword. Down the hill came Goliath bellowing like a berserk bull. He stopped at the water's edge.

Listeners on Point Like a Hunting Dog

> Down from the camp of the Israelites came King Saul, five feet seven inches tall, dressed in armor from head to foot, nothing showing except his two little eyes and his handsome face. In the scabbard at his side swung his eight-pound sword. Down the hill came King Saul, walking very quietly. He stopped at the water's edge.
>
> "I challenge you, King Saul, to fight me to the death!" roared Goliath. "If you kill me my people shall be your slaves for life. If I kill you your people shall be my slaves for life. To the death, King Saul!"
>
> Said King Saul, "You wait right where you are," and back he went up the hill to the camp of the Israelites, who gathered in a huddle about their leader.
>
> "Who will kill Goliath," said Saul, "and save us all from slavery?"
>
> There was silence in the multitude.
>
> "Whoever kills Goliath shall be acclaimed our National Champion forevermore. Who will kill Goliath?"
>
> There was silence in the multitude.
>
> "Whoever kills Goliath shall marry my full-bosomed daughter, Michele. Who will kill Goliath?"
>
> *There was silence in the multitude . . .*

The warning light flashes, Mr. Persuasive Speaker! Do something right now or you will lose that audience! Your picture is losing its movement and without movement curiosity goes dead and attention goes sick. *Start a fight: make your movement lead to a conflict:*

> . .*"I will kill Goliath, sir," said David* . . .

Bang! Now you have it—the *pièce de résistance*, the big struggle, the thrill getter, the conflict—David against Goliath! Everybody loves a good fight. *A fight creates interest.* But you have thrown into this particular fight something that will do more than merely create interest. You have added a fifth dimension that will cement that interest and hold your audience on point like a hunting dog—they will hang in there with you until the last shot is fired: *You have given the conflict an underdog.*

ROCK-THROWING TEENAGER WITH A VISION

People the wide world over feel for the underdog. They want to take his place and they want to take his part. They *identify* with the underdog in his trouble. They become the underdog in their hearts. They actually *are* the underdog—*in their hearts.* They cannot leave your fight because this is now their fight. Each of them is facing Goliath.

Mr. Persuasive Speaker, you have pulled those listeners to the edge of their seats. Now pour it on:

> . . . Look at David. He's just a youngster. He's not a soldier, he's a shepherd boy. The only reason he is here today is that he came over to the camp to bring some cheese and crackers to his three brothers who are soldiers in King Saul's army. He is supposed to return home right now and tend his sheep.
>
> Take a *good* look at David: here is a teenage kid dressed

in a goat skin holding a slingshot in his right hand; wiry as a jungle cat, true, and healthy as a rock, certainly, because he had spent most of his young life on the open range herding his father's sheep—a fine specimen of what a youngster should be physically—but no soldier and surely no match for the ten-foot Goliath who comes fully armed with the best weapons of war and fully seasoned with years of combat experience.

"I will kill Goliath, sir," said David . . .

Certainly your listeners identify with David. They have to. They want to take his place and they want to take his part. They become this astonishing teenager in their hearts. They actually *are* David—*in their hearts*. Get on with it:

> . . . *King Saul was flabbergasted.*
> "Do you actually think you can kill Goliath, boy," he said.
> "Yes, sir, I think I can, sir, because I have a secret weapon he doesn't know about—I can throw rocks better than anybody. I practiced *until I got good at it*. I had to get good at it so I could keep the wolves away from my father's sheep. I think I can kill Goliath, sir." . . .

This youngster was filled with a thing called *confidence*, confidence in his ability to step up to the firing line and face this tough problem, confidence that came to him because *he had practiced a skill until he became good at it and thrilled with it*.

It was his secret weapon.

4

HOW YOUR SPEECH
WILL STAND YOU TALL

Here is what you have done to your audience thus far:

(1) You have painted for them a picture with your words *that got their attention*. You did not start off trying to make them think. Had you done so, many of them would have settled back in their chairs, folded their hands across their full tummies, and said to themselves:

> "I don't think I know what this speaker is trying to communicate to me. Wonder what Susie McGoosie is doing tonight."

Instead you started off with a word picture that your listeners *looked at* with wide-open mental eyes.

> "I see what you are talking about, Mr. Speaker," and

they sat there *looking* for more. So you gave them more because *pictures attract attention.*

(2) You have made the picture move, *arousing their curiosity and sharpening their attention.* The moment a newborn babe becomes aware of his surroundings he is attracted by anything that moves, and all the days of his life his curiosity comes alive whenever things about him move. *Movement arouses curiosity and sharpens attention.*

(3) You have made the movement lead to a conflict, *stimulating their interest and holding their attention on point.* A baby chick hammers its way out of the egg shell, a new butterfly cuts its way out of the cocoon, a human babe comes kicking and squalling into the world—all living things fight their way into existence and keep on fighting until they become strong. The moment they stop fighting they begin to grow weak. One day they die. Such is life: fight and live or surrender and die. Conflict is the very essence of life, all life, animal or plant. To a spectator a good fight "lets it all hang out," *seizing his interest and gripping his attention.*

(4) You have featured an underdog in your fight, thereby *cementing your listeners' interest and locking in their attention* for the duration of the fight. People become intensely wrapped up in anything they can feel for and identify with, and the hapless underdog commands attention from every soul, good soul or bad. This identification with *les miserables* gets a *death grip on each person's interest and glues his attention firm and fast.*

(5) You have slipped the underdog a secret weapon, *giving him confidence and your audience hope* for the coming fight. David has practiced a skill until he became good at it and thrilled with it. He thinks he can kill Goliath. Your audience hopes he does because they are David *in their hearts.*

FREEDOM AND GLORY AND A FULL-BOSOMED GIRL

You need now one last thing—you need to stick David in the heart with a cause for action:

. . . "Boy," said King Saul, still flabbergasted, "do you really have the courage to go against this monster!"

"Oh, yes, sir, I know I have the courage, sir, because I have a cause worth fighting for: *I am fighting to keep us all out of slavery!*"

David looked at his king, he pictured his country in slavery to the Philistines, and he identified with king and country. He wanted to take their place and he wanted to take their part. He became king and country in his heart. He felt something deep in his heart like the point of a knife and the thing he felt was the greatest cause for action that burns in the human heart: Operation Survival.

"I have the courage, sir," he said.

He looked at his countrymen gathered about him and he pictured these countrymen worshipping at his feet with arms upstretched exclaiming:

"Hail to thee, National Champion, forevermore!"

And David felt something deep in his heart like a morning sunrise and what he felt was the second greatest cause for action that burns in the human heart: Operation Recognition.

And he said, "I have the courage, sir."

He looked at the King's full-bosomed daughter, Michele, he pictured himself married to the lovely lady, and he felt something deep in his heart like a covey of startled quail and the thing he felt was the third greatest cause for action that burns in the human heart: Operation Romance.

"I will kill Goliath, sir," he said, and he walked down the hill toward the brook that bubbled in the sunshine.

Goliath stood waiting, big and unbeatable. In David's mind glowed a clear, vivid picture of this thing he was fighting for; in his heart burned an intense desire to fight and win.

David was ready. He bristled with morale. He had a secret weapon that gave him confidence and a cause that gave him courage. David was steeped in *confidence, courage, and cause*, a combination that spells *morale, which explodes into action and gets things done*. David was ready.

Big Bloke Who Had to Be Killed

David stopped at the water's edge. He picked up several smooth stones. He fitted one in his sling and held the others in his left hand. He knew that no matter how good you are at a particular skill you will sometimes miss, and if he missed today he would have to try again—very quickly. He was prepared.

David stepped into the shallow brook and waded across. He went to meet Goliath. Goliath did not move. *He just stood there amazed.*

"Operation what?" thought the giant. "Operation Survival? I wonder if anybody wants to tell me that my survival is being threatened by this teenage kid with his slingshot. Hogwash!

"Operation Recognition? I wonder if anybody wants to inform me that my countrymen will gather around me and hail me as their National Champion forevermore for killing this shepherd boy. Pig slop!

"Operation Romance? I wonder if anybody wants to convince me that the pretty girls of the Kingdom will gather around me and stroke my beard and beg me for a little loving after I have snuffed out this youngster. Nonsense! Operation Zilch!"

Splat! David's stone struck Goliath squarely between the eyes, and both those big orbs popped forth like billiard balls. The giant tottered backward for a couple of steps. Then he leaned slowly to the left and then slowly to the right. Then he fell forward flat on his foolish face, gave three spasmodic jerks, and died, because David leaped in, loosened the armor, and plunged the big fellow's thirty-pound sword into the mammoth heart.

It was not just that little rock that killed that big bloke—it was the way "that damn kid throwed it!" He hit him in the eye and then he struck him in the heart.

Mr. Persuasive Speaker, it is not just those little words that persuade that big audience—it's the way you throw them: you hit them in the *eye* and then you stick them in the *heart*.

YOUR SECRET WEAPON

Every time you stand up and face a big audience you are David against Goliath, you are an underdog against a top dog, you are one little word-throwing pilgrim against a mob, but *you have a secret weapon—you know the secret of persuasion.* You worked on it until you got good at it and thrilled with it. It has become your *skill*, your source of *power*.

You have a cause worth fighting for because the one thing this poor old wobbly world needs above all else is a thing called leadership, whose chief tool is a wonderful thing called *persuasion*. This is Operation Survival, which is the number one reason you are becoming a Power Speaker.

Every time you stand up and face a big audience you occupy the position of a leader, and if you do a good job, the audience will hail you as a leader when you sit down. This is Operation Recognition, which is the number two reason you are becoming a Power Speaker.

Every time you stand up and face a big audience you will feel a thrill of excitement, which will be a romantic experience for you because there are more ways of being romantic than by making love to the King's full-bosomed daughter. Any thrilling experience is romantic.

"There's an unclimbable mountain. What'll we do about it?"

"Climb the thing!" shouts the Voice of Romance.
"There's the unreachable moon. What'll we do about it?"
"Reach the blessed thing!"
"There's the unbeatable Goliath. What'll we do about him?"
"Hit him in the eye with a rock!"

All these thrilling challenges come booming forth from the alluring Voice of Romance, which is the number three reason you are becoming a Power Speaker.

Survival, recognition, romance—these three—make you do what you are doing and enable you to make others do what you want *them* to do. *Survival* spells *life*. *Recognition* spells *good life*. *Romance* spells *thrilling life*. Together they spell *good, thrilling life*.

LITTLE GIRL FAR FROM LOST

Look at this:

The lovely lady was worried. Her soldier husband Jim was coming home from the war. He had survived. He was alive and well. But standing at the train station, holding the small hand of their little four-year-old daughter, the beautiful woman was worried. Would little Judy recognize her daddy? Probably not, because war makes such strangers of so many fathers. And Jim was sure to be hurt by this lack of recognition.

The train arrived. Here came Jim, grinning from ear to ear and shouting, "Hello da-a-a-ah!"

Judy was a pink and white blur as she broke from her mother's grasp and raced into her daddy's arms. He swung her high. The little girl got a strangle hold on the soldier's neck, then pulled back and gave him the most radiant look he had ever seen in his life.

"Daddy!" she said, "you *did* remember me, didn't you?"

Survival, recognition, romance—these three—spell *good, thrilling life.*

NO OTHER WAY TO PERSUADE THAN THIS

You persuade an audience when you make them feel that doing what you propose will give them a *better, more thrilling life.* There is no other way to persuade anybody to do anything.

After you tell your listeners a story of some David defeating some Goliath, you then show them how they are in the same position as David, how the problem they face is their Goliath, and how they can defeat this particular Goliath by using their secret weapon—their good education or their fine organization or their great public spirit or whatever secret weapon you have figured out for them (everybody has a secret weapon even though nothing more than a chestful of courage)—and how solving this particular problem will give each of them a *better, more thrilling life.*

Their secret weapon gives them confidence. Their cause gives them courage. Confidence, courage, and cause make a magic formula that swings them into action on your proposal.

Here then is the secret of persuasion: with your words paint in the minds of your listeners a picture that moves to a conflict featuring an underdog who has a secret weapon that gives him confidence and a cause that gives him courage; then show your listeners how they are in the same boat as David, show them their secret weapon, hang them up with a basic cause, and hurl your challenge.

This is Power. This is the way to persuade. There is no other way.

5

THE POWER THAT MAKES
YOUR TALK SO STRONG

Mr. Persuasive Speaker, every mother's son in that big audience wants to "be his own man." If you have done a good job with your persuasive speech, each listener will come away mulling your proposal over in his mind.

"I think," he says to himself or to his neighbor, "that I will do what this speaker suggests."

He *thinks*. *He* thinks. You made him *feel* and his feelings made him *think*. He thinks he will do this thing that you suggest, but doing it will be *his* decision, not yours. He will give you credit for painting a good picture that made him *see* the problem and *feel* the need for action, but he'll give himself credit for *thinking* about it and *deciding* upon it. He'll give you credit for being a *very smart leader* but he'll give himself credit for being a *man of decision*.

You made his adrenalin squirt, you set him on fire, you made him *feel*, his *feelings* made him *think*, and he *thinks* he will *do* what you suggest, but it's *his* thinking and *his* decision, not yours.

So he shakes your hand and tackles your proposal with great pride. You built up his confidence, you built up his courage, but he built up his own pride, and "he is his own man."

In this Land of the Pilgrim's Pride where we forevermore clamor for freedom for the individual, you cannot make a man do something he doesn't want to do. You can throw a gun on him and make him give you his money, but just let him suspect that your gun is made of wood and he'll knock your teeth down your throat. But you can make him want to donate that same money so that he'll donate it cheerfully and brag about it afterward as if the whole thing were his own idea all along. Persuasion uses a great power, a psychological thing called suggestion, the wonderful power of suggestion. It works!

GETTING THE JUICES TO OVERFLOW

If some happy-go-lucky rascal comes traipsing before you sucking a sour lemon, your salivary glands will squirt and your face will pucker because your feeling-brain, which can't *think* but can *see* and loves to watch television, will *look* at the clear, vivid picture of the lemon sucker showing on your mental view graph and will *feel* that you are the one sucking the lemon and will set your juices flowing.

This is suggestion. It really works!

MAKING THE ENERGY SQUIRT

If you see a man drowning in a river, your feeling-brain will look at the clear, vivid picture and feel that you are the one drowning and will send you a burst of fresh energy for getting yourself out of that big, fast-flowing river.

The drowning man is David. The river is Goliath and Goliath is winning this fight. You identify with the underdog. You have a secret weapon—you're a good swimmer because you practiced a skill until you got good at it and thrilled with it. You have a cause worth fighting for, Operation Survival, because you have identified with the drowning man His fight is your fight.

Your confidence flashes a green light on the television screen of your thinking-brain. Your feeling-brain vibrates. It sends a quick message down to the emotions saying, *"Sock it to 'em, knock 'em down, hit!"* You hit the water, swim out to the drowning man, grab him by his hair, haul him to the bank, throw him out on the grass and lie there beside him exhausted, but happy. Happy because today you made that old devil river give up two human hearts.

During the rescue a continuous flow of fresh energy kept surging through your muscles because your feeling-brain felt all the while that you were the drowning man and kept your hot line burning with the message: *"Sock it to 'em, knock 'em down, hit!"*

This is the power of suggestion I say it works!

SETTING A LISTENER ON FIRE

If you tell a listener a David and Goliath story and get him to identify with David, then his feeling-brain will feel that he actually is David going forth to fight Goliath and will squirt the adrenalin into his blood stream that will set him on fire and get him ready to tackle vhatever problem you plan to throw at him in place of Goliath

Such is the wonderful power of suggestion, the secret weapon of persuasion. Man how it works!

PINNING DOWN THE SECRET

The secret of Power Speaking, then, finally bubbles itself down to three words:

(1) *Picture*, which presents the problem.

(2) *Identification*, which gets the listener involved.

(3) *Suggestion*, which incites the listener to action.

6

NOBLE KNIGHT OF POWER SPEAKING

Do you know what I admire most about you, Mr. Power Speaker? You never *argue* with anybody—except one person. When you stand up to speak you put the audience on your team. You and that audience are fighting for the same thing, a better, more thrilling life. They like you because you have come to them and are showing them a better way to go. You like them because they are drawing out the best that is in you.

If you were to allow yourself the luxury of arguing with some argument-loving challenger, he would square off right then and become your opponent right there. He would make himself David and you Goliath. You would make yourself David and him Goliath. That's pretty silly because the fight would then be David against David and nobody would win, although each of you afterward would give himself credit for the victory. Not one blessed thing would have been accomplished. How silly can we get? Thank goodness you don't argue with anybody—except one person.

SQUELCHING A LAPEL GRABBER

If after your speech some sad soul from the audience comes scampering forward, grabbing your coat lapels, and ranting and raving about what a good Christian he is and how he doesn't like what you said about David making love to the King's full-bosomed daughter because David was a fine, moral young man who later became the great King David and Michele was a saintly young lady who became the Queen, both of them beloved by all the people, let the man blow off steam. Listen to him.

Just blowing off steam will solve his problem halfway. Everybody wants his opinion respected. Anybody with a complaint is looking for sympathy. Always pride is at stake. So let him "be his own man." Nod a bit now and then under his steady fire. Never shake your head at anything he says. Repeat after him some of his more scathing blasts and repeat them in *clear*, *distinct* syllables so that he can hear his own words bouncing back at him off your manly chest. Most grievances are imaginary. All of them are exaggerated. When his scorching tirade comes boomeranging back, he recoils at its vehemence and begins to ease up because you are *not arguing*.

What you really feel like doing to this obstreperous lapel grabber is mash him with your bony fist right in the "china closet and knock a few cups and saucers down into his bread basket." But if you ever do that, you will have to turn in your union card because you will have forfeited your membership in *The Noble Knights of Power Speaking*.

WORDS THAT BOUNCE AND BOOMERANG

Take a look at this bit of persuasion:

One day a mother spanked her little son and he went scream-
ing off out-of-doors.
"I hate you—hate you—hate you!" he cried at the top
of his lungs.
Back from a cliff across the way bounced the youngster's
falsetto tones clear and distinct:
"I hate you—hate you—hate you!"
The little fellow's eyes popped wide open, and he scrambled
back into the house and cried:
"Mother, some old man out there hates me!"
The mother took her offspring by his tiny hand and led
him back outdoors. Facing the cliff, she said:
"Son, yell this: *I love you—love you—love you.*"
The boy yelled the words. Back from the cliff, clear and
distinct, boomeranged the echo:
"*I love you—love you—love you.*"
"This is the law of life, my boy: *what we give we get
back in return.*"

Mr. Power Speaker, 'tis also the *law of Power Speaking:*
Give them understanding, respect their right to disagree, admire
their courage in firing point-blank back at you and tell them
so, but the next time you get up to speak, pour it on the way
you did before—*hit them in the eye and stick them in the heart.*

CRANKING UP AND BLASTING OFF

There lives but one person in all the world you should ever
argue with, and you should argue with that rascal vehemently
and often: *the man in the looking glass.* Arguing with yourself

is vital while working out a proposal to present to your audience, while putting a speech together, while selecting your word pictures, while checking the logic of your points, and while balancing advantages against disadvantages.

"To say or not to say—that is the question," so you argue with yourself far into the night over just *what to say*. But once you get it argued out then prepare to crank up and blast off "Sock it to 'em! Knock 'em down! Hit!"—with words, not your bony fist.

A WAY THAT WORKS AND GETS THINGS DONE

Persuasion is a tool that works and gets things done. Argument is a bludgeon that batters and bruises and gets *nothing* done. Challenge a man to a foot race or a tennis match or a game of mumbletypeg, but don't challenge him to a fight with words unless you are a lawyer in court or a candidate for public office, and even then you prepare yourself to throw words not to knock your opponent down so much as to convince a jury or the voting public to go your way. You use *persuasion*, not *dissuasion*. I wonder how many times you and I have snatched our vote away from some candidate who rose to the podium and scalded his opponent with such torrid phrases that we identified with the mistreated fellow. We wanted to take his place and we wanted to take his part, so we went striding to the polls and rammed down the lever for him instead.

I chased a vacuum sweeper salesman out of my house one day even though I really wanted to buy his machine. But he kept criticizing the company that made the old sweeper I was turning in so that I identified with the mistreated company and went out and bought a new model like my old one.

If you overhear one of your friends declaring that Bucky Walters pitched the Cincinnati Redlegs to victory over the New

York Yankees in the 1940 World Series and you refute him by claiming it was the Detroit Tigers, not the Yankees, you are not challenging your friend to a fight with words, not really, but trying to establish the truth. However, your friend will not have it your way and you will not have it his way. So what do you do, sit there and argue about it?

No sir. You bet each other five dollars and shake hands and go to the record book. The loser pays off, and you shake hands again, and the thing is settled. It's good clean fun, not argument, because argument tries to batter the opponent into helplessness, to hammer him into submission, to make him cry uncle. No real, dyed-in-the-wool argumentator will ever cry uncle. He has a thing going for him called bull-headed stubbornness and the only way to shut him up is to knock him down with your bony fist.

Arguments cannot be settled, only compromised. *That's your cue,* Mr. Power Speaker: corner those two word-bombing sharp shooters, show them how much you admire their fighting spirit, get each side to concede a point or two, and end up with a handshake all around. Neither side wins but the compromise makes life more livable because both sides escape defeat and there is a trace of *camaraderie* in the handshake and smiles that follow, all of which contribute to survival, recognition, and romance, thus adding a bit to a better, more thrilling life for all concerned. And, when meeting time rolls around again, the Noble Knights of Power Speaking will present you their Silver Tongue Medal for valor shown in the face of futility. Persuasion, not dissuasion. This is *Power.*

7

LIGHT-HEARTED WORDS
THAT COME HAMMERING HOME

The man who grabbed your coat lapels because of your frivolous phrasing of the David and Goliath story probably had something special going for King David in his lodge work or his Bible class. Somewhere in every audience sits somebody uptight with a pet peeve about something. If you happen to hit his hot button, you may lose him, but no persuader yet has ever won them all. A simple majority rallying to your proposal should please you well, and a big majority should tickle you half to death.

When you use light-hearted words sincerely to hammer home a serious proposal you hit your listeners with a powerful technique called *contrast*. Mr. Persuader, underline these words in bold black ink: *contrasts pack a wallop*.

Little David and big Goliath are eye-popping contrasts, but

your light-hearted words sincerely spoken and hammered home with a heavy-laden lesson come across as a heart-throbbing contrast that is one of persuasion's most powerful techniques. All great comedies hit you hard with serious themes. The circus clown who makes you laugh works with tears in his eyes. Abraham Lincoln during the darkest hours of the Civil War punctuated his cabinet meetings with funny stories, and his frivolous words leaped across the table with an impact that went deep and stuck fast.

Whether you make your listeners laugh or cry or tingle or any two or all three, they like you. When they laugh, you made them feel good—they liked it. When they cry, you opened your heart to them—they liked it. When they tingle, you thrilled them—they loved it. Whether they laugh, cry, or tingle, you steer a collison course straight into their hearts. Never forget this: every human heart harbors three vessels that carry the causes for all motivated action—*survival, recognition, romance.*

Haul up the anchor, Persuasive Mate, and prepare to embark on a voyage:

Seven Pretty Powerful Girls

We took our Big Ten Football Champions out to California a while back to play the University of Southern Cal in the Rose Bowl, a game that would determine whether we or the Californians were National Champions for the year. Southern Cal was loaded with seniors making their third straight trip to this famous Tournament of Roses. Wise in the ways of post-season play and led by O. J. Simpson, voted the finest college football player during the decade of the Sixties, the Trojans of the Far West were the Goliath of the college football world.

Our Ohio State team was composed mostly of sophomores, "youngsters hardly dry behind the ears yet, with their mother's last kiss still fresh on their lips" going into their first bowl game ever. Here was David sauntering forth

to meet Goliath. *But we had a secret weapon:* we had
a Power Speaker in charge of the trip, a fellow we called
the Big Man, whose way with words got wondrous results.

As we were coming down the gang plank from the airplane at Los Angeles Airport, a motorcycle policeman with
sirens sounding came storming upon the grounds leading
a long string of white limousines, about three dozen
altogether, brand new, each of them emblazoned on either
side with a big red rose. This motor caravan stopped alongside our airplane, and the doors of the first seven limousines
flew open and from each sprang a beautiful girl dressed
in a little red mini-skirt. These seven little ladies were simply
lovely. They were the Rose Bowl Queen and her court of
six princesses. They came running toward us with their arms
outstretched that cute way girls have of wiggle-hipping
toward you when they are tickled to see you.

"Welcome to California, fellows," they said.

Man! Our fellows loved it. Remember, our squad was
mostly green country boys not yet acquainted with the ways
of the world romantic. They did not know what these pretty
girls wanted, but they were certainly willing to find out.

"Get into the limousines, fellows," said the Queen, "and
we'll take you to your hotel and show you a good time."

Wow! We had fifty players on the Rose Bowl squad, plus
ten coaches, eight trainers, six managers, four team doctors,
and a number of administrators—eighty men altogether—all
healthy fellows thoroughly drilled in survival, recognition, and
romance, except for our youthful warriors of the gridiron, who
were just beginning to catch on to life but coming fast with
a good, strong grip.

You should have seen all eighty of those healthy male
animals trying to squeeze into the first seven limousines. Then
the Big Man stepped forward and took charge.

"Hold it!" he shouted. "I want Red One" (our starting
offensive team) "and the Bucks" (our starting defensive team)
"and the head coach" (him) "to get into the first seven cars,
and the A-Y-O's" (all you others) "to bring up the rear."

The Big Man was using some light-hearted words *but he
spoke them sincerely and he was taking charge,* so we piled

into the limousines and cavalcaded down the main thoroughfares of Los Angeles to the Huntington-Sheraton Hotel in the beautiful foothills of Pasadena. The television people came over, the girls threw oranges at the football players, those stalwart devils fired the fruit at the coaches, and we made a few speeches. It was a great day.

Jumping and Bubbling and Eager for Action

Next morning about 7:30 while we were finishing breakfast, into the lobby of the hotel came those seven pretty girls, jumping up and down and bubbling from top to bottom.

"Climb into the limousines, fellows," they said. "We're going to take you to Disneyland and show you a good time."

We spent the whole day promenading through Disneyland alongside those seven little lovelies, ending with dinner that evening, compliments of Mr. Disney's organization. It was a great day.

Next morning right after breakfast here came those girls again still jumping and bubbling.

"Get into the limousines, fellows. We're going to take you to Universal Studios and show you a good time."

We went to Universal Studios, had lunch with some of the actors and actresses, and took part in a movie. They were doing a scene from *The Virginian,* where a poor horse thief was getting himself lynched. They wanted us to be part of the mob. They gave us ten-gallon hats, stuck us in the middle of the crowd, and told us to make some noise. We jumped up and down and shook our fists high in the air and yelled, "We will overcome!" It was a great day.

The next morning at 7:30 right after breakfast, the Queen and her court, as full of bounce as ever, came again.

"Get into the limousines, fellows. We're going to take you out for a day at the beach and show you a good time."

Do you think our fellows wanted to go to the beach with those pretty girls? Right! They jumped up. They were ready to ride. But the Big Man stepped forward. *He took charge.*

"Hold it!" he shouted. "Girls," he said gently, 'you

are nice, you are sweet, you are lovely. We appreciate everything you are doing for us. But we won't be going to the beach. We have work to do. Goodbye.''

The girls left.

"Nice" and "sweet" and "lovely" are light-hearted words *but they were spoken sincerely* and the Big Man *was taking charge.*

The telephone rang. Somebody wanted to talk to the Big Man.

"Coach," said the manager of one of the most world-famous restaurants in downtown Los Angeles, "we have just loaded our refrigerator with five hundred pounds of the best beef steak money can buy. Bring that football team of yours down here tonight and let us fill them up with the best protein they ever ate in their lives. It's on the house, Coach."

"Thank you, mister," said the Big Man. "You are very nice and we appreciate it, but we won't be down tonight or any other night. We'll be coming in tired from football practice on aching dogs that will not hunt. We'll just relax around the hotel until our meal is ready here. We'll buy our own dinner, thank you."

"Aching dogs that will not hunt" is a frivolous phrase *but it was spoken sincerely by a man taking charge.* We paid $700 for that evening meal. We paid $700 for *every* evening meal. We could have had that one for free.

PULSATIONS FROM THE LAND OF ROMANCE

Mr. Power Speaker, do you read the action? Do you see what was happening? Do you think the techniques of persuasion were at work on us out there in the Golden West? Right. No human being ever treated any other human being any nicer than those wonderful people of Pasadena treated us the two weeks we were there getting ready to play that Rose Bowl game. But how well do you read the action?

Take a look at it backwards:

Operation Romance? Definitely. And from the pulsating

heart of romance—Hollywood, with its exotic environs. Yes, romance for sure.

Operation Recognition? True. For those nice people stuck us high on a pedestal and flocked from afar bringing beefsteak, frankincense, and pretty girls. Yes! recognition, no question.

Operation Survival? *No, absolutely not.* Those sweet loving people of Pasadena were setting us up for the kill! Inadvertently, of course, but preparing our little lambs for the slaughter nevertheless. They were about to get us fat in the head and plump in the rump:

> If you rope a wild hog and try to drag him out of the jungle, he'll kill you. But corral that ferocious beast and feed him for a month and pat him on the head and whisper in his ear, and he'll follow you out of the jungle—*fat in the head and plump in the rump.*

Only one thing saved our youngsters from getting fat-headed and plump-rumped: we had a Power Speaker in charge of our trip. He overpowered those pulsating persuaders of the Golden West. Do you know the secret of his power? *His way with words!*

> . . . So the pretty girls stopped coming in the morning right after breakfast—they started coming in the evening right after dinner. They chatted with our young men and strolled with them around the lovely grounds of the Huntington-Sheraton Hotel.
>
> At 10:25 the Big Man stepped into the courtyard and shouted, "Hear this, Ohio State football player: It's 10:25. At 10:30 each of you men will be upstairs, each man in his own room, each in his own bed—alone—with the lights out. Girls, it's been swell. Goodnight." The Big Man spoke his speech with a smile *but he spoke sincerely and he spoke like a man taking charge.*
>
> The girls left and the boys went upstairs. At 10:30 we, the nine assistant coaches, checked them into bed. When we

were finished the Big Man stepped into the darkness of each room, smashed his fist into the wall three times, and shouted, "Sock it to 'em, knock 'em down, hit!" Then he switched on the light.

"Good night, National Champions," he said—*very sincerely*.

"Goodnight, Coach," said the would-be National Champions.

Then the Big Man switched off the light and went to the next room.

The following morning as we sat at the breakfast table waiting for our bacon and eggs, the Big Man came in. He smashed his fist down hard upon the nearest table three times. He punctuated his fisticuffs with his favorite theme song:

"Sock it to 'em, knock 'em down, hit!" These are frivolous words really. But he held in front of him a clinched fist and said, "Good morning, National Champions." This was the manner *of a sincere man taking charge*.

"Good morning, Coach," said the would-be National Champions.

"You football players wanted to go to the beach yesterday with those pretty girls, didn't you?"

"Yes, sir," murmured the players.

"You assistant coaches wanted to go too, didn't you?"

"Yes, sir," murmured the assistants.

"That proves one thing," said the Big Man. "You're human. Well, men, I'm human, too. There's nothing in the world I would rather do than go to the beach with those pretty girls—except one thing: *win the National Championship*.

"Gentlemen, we will not be going to the beach. We'll be going to the football field once in the morning and again in the afternoon—that's twice a day—every day we're here. We came to do a job. We'll get that job done!" *He spoke sincerely like a man taking charge.*

Salutation with a Message

On Tuesday, the day before the game, we practiced only once in the morning and went at noon down town to a press luncheon honoring our coaching staff, the Southern Cal staff, our captains, their captains, and about a thousand sports writers from all over America. The sports writers were the audience and the rest of us were the program. We sat at the head table with a microphone and a master of ceremonies. The program consisted of any of the sports writers picking out a sucker at the head table and asking him a question about the coming game.

The best question of the afternoon and the most exciting answer came when Jim Murray, typewriter athlete of the *Los Angeles Times*, asked the Big Man to step to the microphone. Murray is a little guy. He could scarcely knock you down with his bony little fist, but he can lay you out cold with his secret weapon, which is a large pulsating typewriter. The Big Man has been his favorite target over the years. The Big Man does not like Jim Murray.

"Coach," said Murray, "what is the one thing you fear most about the Trojans?"

The Big Man came with his hands on his hips. He turned his left side to the microphone. He spread his feet. He glared at Jim Murray. Whenever the Big Man faces you left-sided like that with hands on hips and feet spread, he doesn't like you and has taken his favorite position to get to you quickly with *his* secret weapon, a hard left to the jaw, which is a pretty good punch because he is left-handed and puts two hundred forty pounds behind the blow

Of course Murray out in the middle of a thousand people was entirely safe.

"I don't fear *one damn thing* about the Trojans, fellow!" bellowed the Big Man.

"But, Coach, down there at the end of the table sits O. J. Simpson, the finest football player in America throughout the past ten years!"

"Salutations to you, O. J. Simpson," said the Big Man, saluting the Southern Cal captain, "and a message, young man: tomorrow afternoon we're going to *sock it to you, knock you down, hit you, lad!*"

The audience laughed but the Big Man *seemed very sincere and he looked like a man taking charge.* O. J. Simpson rose to his feet, good-looking, polite, raised in the ghetto (which proves one thing: you can raise them anywhere if you raise them right) and returned the Big Man's salute.

"Salutations to you, Coach Hayes, and a message, sir: tomorrow afternoon you'll have to *catch me first!*"

The audience laughed again, but O. J. *seemed very sincere and he looked like a man already in charge.* This young man could do the dash in 9.4 and the best we could do was 9.8. We would have to hurry.

Energy and Spirit and Blood

The next afternoon during the first seventeen times "Orange Juice" Simpson carried the football, we hit that halfback with every ounce of our energy and every spark of our spirit and every drop of our blood. We did everything to that young man but nail him to the cross the first seventeen times he carried the ball. Then came Simpson for the eighteenth time.

The ball was on the Southern Cal twenty-yard line, eighty yards deep in the hole and way out of trouble—we thought. O. J. started wide to the left running like a two-legged antelope, took a pitchout from his quarterback, cut back inside Marc DeBevic and Doug Adams and Jim Stillwagon and Tim Anderson and Mike Sensibaugh and Jack Tatum, leveled off toward the goal line, stuck his nose toward the west, thrust his long legs into high gear, and away he went up the glory road into the promised land—with seven points for the Trojans. Only one thing could possibly have stopped that high-stepping halfback on his beautiful eighty-yard run for the Roses—the Pacific Ocean. We were in trouble.

We pulled our defensive team from the field and put in

the offense. The defense did not sit down. They gathered in a circle about their coach. You could not see the Big Man except for his fists reaching high in the air and coming down hard on the shoulders of his players. He did not hit the youngster—he popped his pads. He presented *a very sincere picture of a man taking charge*, as he reached high and came down hard on the pads of his players. Those shoulder pads are terrific. The player feels nothing physical; however, the picture of the pulsating man and the sound of the popping pads gets his attention.

"Do you see what happens when you don't *sock it to him, knock him down, hit!*" roared the Big Man.

"Yes, sir," murmured the players.

Thirty-six times that afternoon O. J. Simpson carried that football. Thirty-five times we socked it to him and knocked him down and hit that fine young man all over that Rose Bowl field. We won the football game 27-16.

ONE THING ABOVE ALL ELSE

Do you know why we won that Rose Bowl Game and the National Championship and got ourselves selected as the greatest college football team during the decade of the 60's? Because we took with us to California the one thing this country needs more than anything else in all this world, a Power Speaker. Do you know what gave our Power Speaker so much power? His way with words. Woody Hayes knows a lot about the game of football, but that's not it. With only a little football know-how he still would have led us to victory in that Rose Bowl game because the man has mastered one of Power Speaking's greatest techniques: *he knows how to use light-hearted words sincerely to hammer home a serious proposal in the manner of a man taking charge.*

Mr. Power Speaker, no matter whether you are right or

wrong on the proposal with which you are challenging your audience, if you *think* you are right and *feel* in your bones you are right and use light-hearted words and breathe sincerity into your voice, your feeling-brain will feel that you are truly right and will send you a burst of fresh energy and a surge of new ideas that will give you the poise and bearing of a man who knows what he is talking about. Here's the amazing thing about it: even though your audience may not agree with you on this particular proposal, *the sincere picture you cut as you stand there speaking like a man taking charge* will get snatched away from the thinking-brains of your listeners by their feeling-brains and rushed off below the surface of their awareness, and they will feel a burst of confidence in you and a surging idea that they should follow you as a leader.

Why? Because your light-hearted words made them *feel* good—disarming their doubting minds. Your sincere manner made them *identify* with you—made them want to take your part—and your take-charge attitude drew them to your side—just like Woody Hayes' football players rallying behind their leader in the Rose Bowl.

You have been working with the *wonderful power of suggestion*—remember?

Hips That Wiggle and Arms That Reach

The day after the Rose Bowl game, we gathered in the lobby of the Huntington-Sheraton Hotel prepared to head back to Ohio State University and start hitting the books again. But the Big Man stepped into the middle of the lobby, held up his hand, and called for attention.

"Gentlemen," he said, "we'll not be going home today; we'll wait until tomorrow—we have some unfinished business to take care of."

The next moment into the lobby of the hotel sprang seven

pretty girls, holding forth their arms that cute way girls have when they come wiggle-hipping toward you tickled to death to see you.

"Get into the limousines, fellows," said the Queen. "We're going to take you out for a day at the beach and show you a good time."

We went. It was a great day.

8

PRIMING THE POWER MECHANISM

There will come a time in your life, Mr. Power Speaker, when you will find it necessary to unload both barrels of your power mechanism right between the listener's eyes. Your greatest virtues are your ability to stand up before criticism and give back understanding to feelings you have hurt, patience at tirades against your light-hearted treatment of somebody's pet character, and admiration for any show of spirit against your proposal. You firmly hold your ground and permit such criticism to boomerang upon the poor listener who is clutching at straws as he seeks desperately "to be his own man."

All living things must struggle for a better, more thrilling life, and all Power Speakers identify with any pulsating creature who puts up a good struggle—win, lose, or draw. Those who struggle and win we congratulate for their victory. Those who struggle and lose we compliment for their fight. Those who perish in the struggle we eulogize in song and story and statue. Three everlasting cheers for any living creature that will stand up and fight for a better, more thrilling life—*this is what it's all about!*

WAKING UP THE HO-HUM BRIGADE

But tonight, yonder sits a horde of people known as the silent majority. These are the shoulder-shruggers, the do-nothings, the ho-hum brigade, who sit through your speech nodding their heads in agreement and applauding politely at your conclusion but who will now go sallying forth into the night exclaiming what a fine proposal yours is and how somebody ought to do something about it but who will never lift a finger to do one solitary thing about it themselves. They liked your speech though. They think you are a fine fellow. They shake your hand and tell you so. If you were not a Power Speaker you would go home satisfied—fat in the head and plump in the rump.

Since they liked your speech you will get a chance to come again and address that same group. The next time you come you will stand up with both barrels loaded. You will throw down on that phlegmatic mass of shoulder-shrugging do-nothings and pull both triggers at once. You will get mad. You will blow your top. You will flip your lid. Anger is a wonderful fuel for priming a speaker's power mechanism, provided he is careful with his blast-off.

Go ahead and pound your palm and smack the podium and rend the air. Get just as mad as you can possibly get. But, warning, Mr. Power Speaker! Don't hit the listener with your bony fist or a ballbat or a double-barrel peashooter. Actually you have but one legitimate missile to hurl at those sleepy-eyed galoots—*Words*. As a persuader your purpose is to hit them in the *eye* and stick them in the *heart* and *motivate* them to

action on your proposal. But 99 percent of all people who get
mad kick a listener in the *stomach* with their words. They stick
a long skinny finger under his nose and tell him what a miserable
mess he is. That hits him hard in the *stomach*. If you kick a
listener in the stomach with your words, he knows right then
and there exactly what his problem is: *You* are *his* problem,
and he will do one of two things—he'll either fight you or he'll
run away. One thing for sure he will *not* do; he will *not* buy
your proposal.

If he fights you and you lick him, he'll admit he is a miserable
mess, not worthy of your time or anybody else's because he
stinks. He doesn't like himself. He doesn't like you either because
you made him stink. He doesn't like anybody because he thinks
maybe everybody stinks. Mr. Speaker, you have lost that listener
forevermore. You will never persuade that fellow to do anything.
You lost him when you killed his spirit by *kicking him in the
stomach with your words.*

If he fights you and licks you—which can happen—then
you are a miserable mess and you have blown your last chance
with that individual. He's got you in the palm of his hand and
he'll handle you from this day forward.

If he refuses to fight you and runs away, you will have
to go find him and bring him back before you can ever hope
to persuade him. He can run away without ever leaving his seat
just by clamming up and shutting you out so that you couldn't
get his attention now if you pried him open with a crowbar.
All this if you kick a shoulder-shrugging, do-nothing audience
in the *stomach* with your words.

How then does a speaker use his anger as a fuel for his
motivator? Simple. Instead of sticking your finger in their faces
and calling them a miserable mess, you point that digit at the
blank wall on one side of the room and paint them a clear,
vivid picture of *the miserable mess they made* by not moving

on your proposal. You are in essence standing beside them now shoulder to shoulder, man to man, on the same team, fighting for the same thing. But so far you are the only one who's done any fighting. You want them to help you kill Goliath. But you are not begging, you are not pleading, you are not whining, you are booming out a challenge.

PALM-POUNDING PODIUM SMACKER

So with every ounce of your energy and every spark of your spirit you pound your palm, you smack the podium, you rend the air, you hammer them with the one-two-three punch:
  1. Motivate
  2. Accelerate
  3. Re-motivate

You motivate: Paint in their minds a clear, vivid, sparkling, crackling picture of the thing they were supposed to be doing all this time. You tried this the last time you spoke to them, but it didn't work. Now you are mad, and anger is a great fuel for priming a speaker's power mechanism. So you burn your picture on the brains of that sleepy-eyed audience. You drive it into their hearts. You sear it on their souls. You motivate!

And you accelerate: With that same palm-pounding, podium-smacking, air-rending gusto, you paint for these people a picture of the miserable mess they have made by not acting on your proposal, and you use colors so vivid that they recoil from the mess they made—here comes contrast packing its power ful wallop—and they start bouncing in the opposite direction, which is toward the thing you have been proposing all along. This is double-barrel persuasion, recoiling from one thing and bouncing toward the opposite. This is persuasion accelerated by contrast powered by anger carefully applied. You accelerate!

Then you re-motivate: Repeat your proposal, hurl the new challenge, and get out of there. Let them get up and go to work on your proposal or sit there and stew in their own juice.

Here's what you did tonight: You got mad, but you did not kick your listeners in the *stomach*. You did your dead-level best to stick them in the *heart*. If they don't come alive now, pray for their souls and get out of there with your head held high and go on to another audience.

Driving a Listless Group to Greatness

Three days before we played Southern Cal in the Rose Bowl, we were running through our final hard practice getting ready for the game. You have to win a football game twice. You win on Wednesday on the practice field, or you suffer on Saturday in the stadium. You go all out on Wednesday, lick your wounds on Thursday, ooze a little perspiration on Friday, and dash into the stadium on Saturday primed for victory.

But New Year's came on Wednesday. So Sunday had to be our last day for hard practice. The California sun was pouring straight down, heavy on our heads. The Los Angeles smog had drifted in and was clinging low to the practice field. Our players felt miserable wrapped in fourteen pounds of playing equipment. We had just recently flown in from Columbus, Ohio, where there was snow on the ground. It was hot in California. *Our boys were loafing.*

The Big Man stood this phlegmatic workout for five minutes. Then he got mad. He called the squad together in the middle of the practice field and he popped a few shoulder pads. He hit those youngsters hard with hot words, but in the *eye* and in the *heart*, not in the *stomach:*

"Southern California . . . in the Rose Bowl . . . for the National Championship . . . *and you're* LOAFING! YOU ARE LOAFING! *One hundred thousand people in the stands all about us watching us, the Ohio State Buck-eyes . . . one hundred million more all about this nation sitting with their eyes glued to their television sets watching us,*

the Ohio State Buckeyes, going for the National Champ-
ionship . . . and you're blowing our chance! You're
LOAFING! YOU ARE LOAFING!

"Foley! Worden! Come here . . . right here
. . . beside me!" Foley was Captain Dave Foley, six foot
five inch, two hundred sixty pound tackle, who could have
sneezed and blown Woody Hayes right out of that stadium.
Worden was Captain Dirk Worden, six foot two inch, two
hundred ten pound linebacker, who probably could have licked
Woody by circling to the left and slipping the Big Man's first
punch.

"Captain Foley! Captain Worden! *Tell them* WHAT WE
HAVE TO DO!"

The Senior Co-Captains, the old men of the squad, stood
in the center of the circle of sophomores and let their eyes
pan once about the circle. This was the gang of adrenalin-
squirting upstarts who had grabbed the Big Ten Title and had
come storming to the West Coast hungry for the National Championship. Today they were hungry for nothing. They were loafing.
This was certain defeat simmering on the practice field.

The youngsters looked at the oldsters. The oldsters looked
at the youngsters. Said the oldsters at the top of their lungs:

"SOCK IT TO 'EM, KNOCK 'EM DOWN, HIT!"

For the next hour and a half, those young men went at
each other hammer and tongs, tooth and toenail, and when the
day was over they wobbled into the locker room on "aching
dogs that could no longer hunt." The next day they licked their
wounds, the following day they oozed a little perspiration, and
on New Year's Day they went into the Rose Bowl and got
what they came for.

"The greatest college football team during the decade of
the 60's," said Bud Wilkinson and his sports committee.

The President of the United States came to the locker
room and congratulated the team, shaking hands with the man
who had *used anger the Power way as a persuasive technique.*

A Few Little Words Plus a Light-Hearted Clause

The Big Man motivated his players with two words, *National Championship*, which brought back to their minds a clear, vivid picture of the thing they had been fighting for all fall. He accelerated that motivation with three words, *You are loafing*, which brought to their minds a picture of the worst thing that can happen to a football player, a horrible thing called *defeat*. These two pictures bumped into each other in a stirring contrast that caused the players to recoil from the one and bounce toward the other.

He re-motivated his players with a light-hearted clause that carried a heavy-laden message: "Sock it to 'em, knock 'em down, hit!"

TECHNIQUES THAT WORK

Back in Chapter 7 we used light-hearted words sincerely spoken to make a serious point. The contrast packed a wallop. The technique really worked. In this chapter we have used anger sincerely applied to arouse a listless audience. The contrast between what was wanted and what was being done exploded a double-barrel blast in the direction of what was wanted.

If Woody Hayes had kicked his players in the stomach with his words by calling them "miserable loafers whom Southern Cal will murder on New Year's Day," some of the players would have believed him and folded like a two-bit accordion; others would have fought back by going all out against Southern Cal and, had they won the game, just might afterwards have rammed the game ball down the Big Man's throat, which would have made him a miserable mess instead of a great leader. If the Trojans had walloped the Buckeyes, our young sophomores would have gone home feeling that the Big Man had pegged them correctly, a bunch of miserable loafers, a disgrace to the

great game of football; and those youngsters, still coming to
grips with life, would never have gone on to the heights they
reached during the next two years, at the conclusion of which
more of them signed to play pro ball than have the players
of any other college team in all of history.

Shoulder to Shoulder and Man to Man

Woody did not call his players a miserable mess. He stood
beside them, shoulder to shoulder, man to man, fighting for
the same thing, and showed them what they had come to do,
contrasted it with the miserable mess they were making, and
re-stated his challenge. They quit loafing. This is the *Power*
way of using anger.

If you point your nervous finger at me and call me a miserable
mess, I'll say to you, "I can't help it, I was born that way."
But if you stand beside me and show me what a miserable mess
I am making, I'll tell you this:

"One thing I know—I can sure stop making this mess.
Now what do you propose?"

Hit them in the *eye* and stick them in the *heart* but don't
kick them in the *stomach* or the Noble Knights of Power Speaking
will come seeking your union card.

9

NEVER CARESS A LISTENER IN THE STOMACH WITH WORDS

Suppose, Mr. Power Speaker, that you have done such a fine job on an audience that they go rushing forth and get a great job done on your proposal and now throw a banquet to celebrate their achievement. They want you to come again and be their speaker. Naturally you go.

This is a fine group of hard-socking citizens, enough of which could very well save our civilization from going down the drain as did Persia, Egypt, Greece, and Rome, and all other civilizations that ever graced this earth—except ours, so far.

You will want to congratulate these fine people. So you will give them a half-hour speech of praise, but before you sit down you will toss out a strong hint of work still to be done.

"The work of the world is *never* done."

You will caress them gently with a new challenge about which you promise to come and speak later. Promise of a future challenge keeps their feeling-brains churning energy and popping ideas, and when the occasion comes that they again need a speaker, your name will come booming forth from some member of the program committee. Make a good speech of congratulations in which you promise a future challenge and you will stay gainfully employed in the noble field of Power Speaking.

GIVING THEM THE ONE-TWO-THREE PUNCH

Now hear this, Mr. Power Speaker:

In a speech of congratulations you perform exactly the same way you do in any other persuasive speech—you hit them in the *eye* and stick them in the *heart*. But heed this warning: *Don't caress them in the stomach with your words.*

This is a happy occasion. They feel good. You feel good. So go ahead with your speech and show them a better, more thrilling life. *But don't caress them in the stomach with your words!*

If you start off by saying, "You people are absolutely the greatest thing that ever happened to this town or any other town," you are caresssing them in the stomach. You leave them no place to go. If what you say is true, they no longer have anything to fight for in this life because you have given them every-thing—they are the greatest. That leaves them no place to go. Their feeling-brains get goo-goo eyed and flounder and flop. This group of people becomes fat in the head and plump in the rump. Don't caress them in the *stomach*. Hit them in the *eye* and stick them in the *heart*. Don't praise the *audience;* praise their *accomplishment*. Give them the one-two-three punch:

1. Motivate
2. Accelerate
3. Re-motivate

You motivate: recall to their minds the clear, vivid picture of your original proposal.

And you accelerate: compare the thing they did with the thing they were supposed to do. Show them how in one part of the proposal they did a better job than has ever been done before anywhere. Great, great, great! They love that. Show them how in another part they did as well as has ever been done. Good, good, good! They like that. Now show them how in a third part they still need to do a little more work. They will open their eyes wide at that. What other work?

Then you re-motivate: hint at a new proposal you will give them at a future date. Sit down and shut up, and let them enjoy their accomplishment for awhile. They have earned a little rest.

Praising the great job they did, and hinting at a new challenge to come, makes life better and more thrilling for them because their feeling-brains send them a burst of fresh energy and a surge of new ideas for doing other great things. They go from your speech motivated and ready. They await just one thing: a clear, vivid picture of the thing they should be fighting for next. And they will be calling on you for *Power*.

Tallest Hog Around the Trough

Our Sophomore football team that went prancing into the locker room after beating Southern California at the Rose Bowl for the National Championship stood mighty tall in the showers.

When the President had left the locker room and the sports writers came jamming in, the Big Man climbed to the top of a table in the middle of the room and answered questions for the press. The Big Man had come from the field soaking wet with perspiration and the players had tossed him into a cold shower with all his clothes on. The cold shower mixed with the hot sweat. He was a miserable mess.

"Mr. Hayes," said Jim Murray, "is this the greatest football team you ever coached?"

"Don't you print that, fellow!" said the Big Man facing Murray left-sided with hands on hips and feet spread. "You say it like this: This team has done the greatest job on the football field of any team I have ever coached. But you *don't praise the team—you praise the accomplishment!* They are only sophomores. I have to live with them two more years. They still have work to do—great work."

Old Billy Hell and a Lad Called David

Do you suppose those fine football champions got caressed in the stomach during the days that followed? Yes, many, many times and with words that bill and coo. The next year, with only the Michigan game left on the schedule after setting an all-time scoring record for Ohio State football, that surging team of Junior Class college students looked and listened as newspapers and radios and television screens all about the country blared forth the news: *Ohio State has the greatest college football team of all time!"*

On Monday before the Michigan game the athletic office in St. John Arena was flooded with letters, postcards and telegrams, thousands of them, all saying basically the same two things:

(1) Congratulations on being the greatest college football team of all time.

(2) Beat Michigan.

Who in Old Billy Hell is Michigan? If we are the greatest college football team of all time, who in Old Billy Hell is anybody?

A football team fights for victory and yearns for greatness. When they achieve greatness you congratulate them for their accomplishment, but you leave them *somewhere to go.* Our football team had *nowhere* to go. They were already there. They were the greatest. Above that there was nothing—except God.

So Michigan beat us. That defeat knocked the fat off our heads and the plumpness off our rumps.

"You can learn more in defeat than you can in victory but in *one* defeat you can learn it all."

So the next year that team of Seniors, wise now in the ways of the world and the subtleties of life, came storming back for an undefeated season and gave Ohio State the greatest three-year record the school has ever known in football.

Then David came. He drew back his sling and he slew Goliath. David was a youngster by the name of Jim Plunkett, quarterbacking a never-say-die Stanford team that had lost three games that year. Jim Plunkett came with a secret weapon, a rubber arm loaded with an oblong football that he spiraled into the air and set the undefeated Ohio State team down in the '71 Bowl of Roses.

Why? Jim Murray had said before the game, "Woody should have brought his third team to California and let his first two teams go home for Christmas. Using the Ohio State first team against Stanford will be like using a Russian tank to break open an English walnut."

Then David came and hit Goliath in the *eye* and stuck him in the *heart*. One thing Plunkett definitely did not do. He did not caress us in the *stomach* where we had been caressed so many times before.

On the plane heading home after the game the Big Man sat alone, pale and depressed. Sometimes a man's leadership falters and his power fails. The team physician looked at the crestfallen leader and came quickly with stethoscope in hand and checked the Big Man's heart. All the good doctor could hear was: *plunk-ett, plunk-ett, plunk-ett!*

10

THE GREATEST GOLIATH THAT
A SPEAKER FACES

The greatest Goliath that ever a speaker confronts is an audience unfriendly to his proposal. Mr. Speaker, this is your toughest assignment. One way to handle it is to refuse to go—let somebody else make the speech. But sometimes the job falls into your lap and you cannot escape the assignment.

If you sincerely believe in your heart that doing what you propose will give these unfriendly people a better, more thrilling life, then it's worth a good try and your task is to go and make them see it that way. However, if you don't feel your proposal pulsating down in the marrow of your bones, then don't go—let nothing drag you there.

Making a Mob Go Home for Supper

But suppose you are the county sheriff and the angry mob outside has come to lynch Mike Shagnasty for making uncouth love to cute little Susie Magoosie, who is Belle Number One of Calhoun County. Whether Mike is innocent or guilty, he deserves a fair trial, and as the county sheriff you are going to see that he gets it—if you possibly can. So you go striding out and face that angry audience.

First: Even though you may be quaking in your boots, you *put on a show of confidence.* Your feeling-brain will take a quick look at the picture of simple faith that you are cutting and the naive thing will actually feel that you are going to handle this unruly mob and will flood your tingling body with a burst of fresh energy and a surge of new ideas on how to get the job done. Your putting on a show of confidence as you stand up there on the jailhouse steps, David facing Goliath, will also work on the feeling-brains of the aggravated audience so that some of them will marvel at your courage and will unconsciously begin to identify with you in your trouble.

One thing you better know for sure: if you come begging and pleading and whining like some namby-pamby in search of sympathy, your feeling-brain will back off into a dark corner of your cranium and turn off your juices, and those up-tight citizens will stomp on your handsome face as they drag Mike Shagnasty out and hang him to the tallest tree in the county.

Second: *Begin with statements they can't refute.*

Third: *Don't tell them they are wrong; just show them you are right.*

Fourth: *Use some light-hearted words spoken sincerely to make some serious points.*

It's time to start talking:

"You guys got me outnumbered a little bit. . . ."

Actually you are outnumbered about five hundred to one.

Your opening statement shows a contrast built of light-hearted words sincerely spoken to imply a serious point; namely, that you the sheriff are very much an underdog in a life and death situation.

Carry on:

> ". . . But, boys, you elected me sheriff of this county and I promised to enforce the law, and the law says this man gets a fair shake . . ."

Here is a man identifying with his duty and with the people who gave him that duty. No argument here. Give them more:

> ". . . You people are my people—the only people I know—and if you hadn't put me up here I would be down there where you are, feeling the way you feel . . ."

Here are more words of identification that offer no place for the listener to grab hold of and jerk. You are getting stronger, Sheriff:

> ". . . Any of you guys standing up here in my boots would do exactly what I am going to do . . ."

This movement-to-come arouses curiosity and sharpens attention. What is this sheriff going to do? Every member of that lynch mob who happened to be looking at your face, Mr. Sheriff, saw at that moment a new gleam of confidence shining in your eyes. What you yourself saw from your perch on the platform that brought on this added poise was a significant movement in the audience. That movement was going to be your secret weapon. Little David just might handle this Goliath:

> ". . . I'm going to protect this prisoner with my life! You try to take him away from me and you will have a dead

sheriff on your hands . . .''

Greater sincerity hath no man than this, that a man stand ready to lay down his life doing his duty. Maybe you are bluffing, Mr. Sheriff, but you certainly do *sound* sincere and you *look* sincere.

Fifth: *Pop your proposal.* You have said enough. This is no time for a long speech. Sock it to 'em:

". . . You men go on home and eat supper with your wives and kids and let the law of this state handle this prisoner.''

The sheriff has demonstrated to this unfriendly audience a David and Goliath story: Standing up there so all alone, he has cut a picture that moved to a conflict featuring an underdog who came up with a secret weapon (to be explained shortly) that gave him confidence and a cause that gave him courage. *Confidence, courage, and cause—these three—equal morale which explodes into action and gets things done.*

Sixth: *Thank God for the secret weapon* that showed up in this crisis, Mr. Sheriff, for you did not lick this problem all by your lonesome. At least fifty men among that audience of unfriendly folks rose up and helped you get your work done. Otherwise Goliath would have won the day. Whence came this help?

A HELPING HAND FROM ONE OF TEN

Every time you make an effective speech of persuasion to an unfriendly audience, you will get plenty of help because out there sprinkled among those listeners, normally about one out of every ten, will sit (or stand) persuasive people like yourself who don't hesitate to take charge when things get touchy. Anytime you do a good job against an unfriendly audience you will notice people all over the house (or lot) looking away from you and listening to the take-charge fellow in their particular area as he murmurs words of approval and nods approbation at your speech. From your place on the platform you will see this turning and twisting and hear the murmuring through the audience as each section responds to its own particular leader. If you make a clever witticism, they automatically look to their leader to see how he is taking it. If you come zooming across the footlights with a thrill-provoking declaration they turn to their leader to catch his reaction.

In an audience of thousands opposed to your proposal you will pick up strange lieutenants by the hundreds who will help you win that audience over—if you are up there doing a good job. This stirring and murmuring and head-nodding among his irate citizens is what the sheriff saw that brought new confidence to him and acted as a secret weapon that enabled him to pop his proposal boldly and succeed in the most difficult task confronting a speaker.

How does a Power Speaker do a good job with an unfriendly audience? Let's bundle it together like this:

(1) Put on a show of confidence.

(2) Begin with statements they cannot refute.

(3) Don't tell them they are wrong; just show them you are right.

(4) Use some light-hearted words spoken sincerely to make some serious points.

(5) Pop your proposal boldly.

(6) Thank God for the secret weapon that came to your rescue: the natural leaders scattered here and there throughout the audience whom you won over to your side and who then helped you win the others.

TURNING A NO INTO A YES

Suppose you are trying to persuade a friend to go with you on his first camping trip. You know that he will like it if you can just get him there. You feel that he absolutely should go. But he has already said no. So you have an audience of

one who is unfriendly to your proposal. What is your secret
weapon now?

> "It's wonderful up there in the North Woods, paddling
> across the lake under the open sky, sleeping on balsam boughs.
> Every meal is a banquet and you're hungry as a bear. You
> smell the trout sizzling in the pan and you feel the soft breeze
> caressing your cheek. Wow! This is living! This is the good
> life! This is the thrilling life! We can leave tomorrow and be
> back Saturday. Man, let's go!

What secret weapon did you use on this listener? You put
on a show of confidence. You acted as if you knew he was
coming with you to the North Woods. You did not tell him
how wrong he was in staying home. You showed him how right
it was to go. You used light-hearted words, thrilling words, to
picture life in an outdoors camp. Then you boldly popped your
proposal. You and he left at dawn. The secret weapon you used
was a thing called *Power Speaking That Gets Results.*

MISQUOTED AND MISUNDERSTOOD

Somewhere in every audience that you face may sit somebody
who thinks he doesn't like you because of things he has heard
about you. He has never heard you speak but he has heard about
your speeches because you have been getting around, Mr. Power
Speaker, and you are being talked about far and wide. With
all this action going on you are bound to be misquoted and
misunderstood now and then.

DISARMING AN ENEMY AND MAKING A FRIEND

So tonight this unfriendly fellow has come to hear you speak,
prepared to grab your lapels when you are finished. But as usual

you come across with a dandy job of hitting them in the eye and sticking them in the heart, and when it's all over, here comes the obstreperous rascal bounding toward you. You brace yourself and prepare your lapels, but the vivacious fellow grabs your hand, cracks your knuckles, and exclaims, "Man, you're nothing but one hundred per cent okay. I've been misinformed. Somebody told me you were a horse's neck!"

You laugh and thank him and tell him you have been called worse things.

Do you know what won this fellow over to your side more than anything else in your Power speech? He saw the pictures you painted with your words—that's part of the secret, but what was the one technique that pinned him to the mat? He felt the emotions you made him feel when you drove those pictures into his heart—that's the other part of the secret, but what was the technique? His feelings made him think and he thought he just might do something about your proposal. That's what you were after. But what was the one technique that brought it off? *Here it is:* The light-hearted words you spoke sincerely to make a few serious points that he had formerly disagreed with packed a wallop that shook him down to the depths of his soul—*and that is it!* Your light-hearted words disarmed that unfriendly fellow and your sincere manner drew him to your side. You made a lifelong friend tonight. You did it with one of the greatest techniques in power speaking: *Light-hearted Words Sincerely Spoken.*

Actually the science of Power Speaking was used wonderfully well years ago by Napoleon and Hitler and Churchill and way back before them by Demosthenes and others, but the fact that millions of would-be persuaders take thousands of speaking courses every year with only a few hundred Great Persuaders coming out of those classes shouts forth the startling news: Power Speaking is still a new way to verbal persuasion *for most people.* Yet the science is so simple and so easy that it seems silly not to master the thing.

You and I have just finished a thorough discussion on the basic secret of persuasion and several of its more important techniques. Let's settle down now and prepare a persuasive speech and then go out and deliver it.

11

PUTTING YOUR SPEECH INTO ONE UNFORGETTABLE SENTENCE

What do you want this particular audience to do, Mr. Power Speaker? What proposal do you plan to challenge them with? Do you want them to vote or join or donate or write or buy or boycott or enlist or investigate or acquit or convict or what? Do you want them to act right now or later?

I'll vote for your man next Tuesday, I'll donate money for the new jail right now, I'll even buy your old lawnmower whenever you bring it over, *if you can show me that doing these things will give me a better, more thrilling life.* However if you want me to contribute money to replace the delapidated pokey, you will have to paint me a picture of those poor, woe-be-gone inmates and make me identify with them and become them in my heart so that I cannot go from you and live my life in peace until I cross your palm with a bit of hard-earned lucre for the jailhouse cause.

When you have decided the one definite response you want from this particular audience, grab a pencil and paper and *sound your theme!* Cram your entire speech into *one unforgettable sentence!* Call upon your little thinking-brain and sweat out the one solid thought that will carry the message of your whole speech. Make that sentence compact and eye-catching. This is your theme. This is the little thread that will run so true throughout your talk and bind everything you say into one neat bundle. This is the one big idea that will come alive within your listener as you brand it on his brain with pictures and drive it into his heart with a cause for action. This is head stuff that will become heart stuff and explode into soul stuff as your audience rallies behind your proposal. Memorize it. You will not memorize your speech but you will most certainly memorize your theme.

HOW TO WORK WONDERS WITH WORDS

Do you know the theme of this book? I worked on it a long time before I was satisfied with it. Here 'tis: *"The one thing this poor old uptight ball of earth needs above all else is a thing called leadership, whose secret weapon is a thing called persuasion."*

Do you know the response I want from you? I have written three books. I wrote the first one because I wanted football coaches to open up their offense and give the spectators a better, more thrilling game. I wrote the second because I wanted those same coaches to stand tall and lead their young men to a better, more thrilling athletic experience. I am writing this one for you, Mr. Speaker: I want you to become a Great Persuader, a Power Speaker. Why? Because our survival as a civilization depends on persuasion and your survival in a competitive society depends on your ability to persuade—*survival* spells *life.* Our recognition as a world power depends on persuasion and your recognition

as a vibrant human being depends on your ability to persuade—*recognition* spells *good life*. Our romance in science and
invention depends on persuasion and your romance with exciting
audiences depends on your ability to persuade—*romance* spells
thrilling life. Why do I want you to become a Great Persuader?
So that you and all those who sit in your audiences may enjoy
a better, more thrilling life.

GETTING GOOD AT IT AND THRILLED WITH IT

How do you become a Great Persuader? By working on
persuasion until you get good at it and thrilled with it, so good
and so thrilled that you will be able to do wonders using it
as your secret weapon in leading people, because "the one thing
this poor old uptight ball of earth needs above all else is a thing
called leadership, whose secret weapon is a thing called persuasion."

GOING DOWN DEEP RIGHT WHERE THEY LIVE

Suppose your audience is entirely female and your proposal
is: *Down with Women's Liberation*. What is your theme? Bear
in mind that you have to get down deep right where they live;
you have to appeal to survival or recognition or romance or
any two or all three. How about this for a theme: "Woman
is God's loveliest flower, to be cultivated, nourished, and protected by a stodgy gardener called man." Delve now into the
pages of literature, consult Byron, Shelley and Keats, and look
for beautiful pictures that will echo your theme. When you stand
up to speak, caress those pictures gently and send them slipping
downward until they rest in every female heart throughout the
audience. Make their feminine juices flow. Then shout your proposal: "Down with Women's Liberation!"

When your speech is over, if you have done a good job you will stagger from the auditorium covered with lipstick and sweet aroma from here to yonder. This was *Power Speaking, Man!*

A CAVE FULL OF WILDCATS

Suppose your proposal is: *Vote for Bodiddly Brown for sheriff.* You have to work out a theme. Here's one: "Bodiddly Brown is a strong man with a courageous heart and a fine feeling for folks." Now go on from there, Mr. Speaker, and paint me a picture of how Bodiddly Brown dove into a cave full of wildcats and brought Baby Boy Broderick forth unscathed, and I'll come marching to the polls next Tuesday bringing with me every eligible voter in my precinct: "Bodiddly Brown for sheriff!"

THE WINNING WAY OF THE POWER SPEAKER

A theme must have "head stuff" and "heart stuff." It must come reaching across the footlights sounding *easy* and *congenial.* It must be *easy* so that we who listen can grasp it right now. This is "head stuff." It must be *congenial* so that we don't throw up a defense and shut you out before you ever get going good. This is "heart stuff." As you echo your theme in the conclusion of your speech, hopefully it will have become "soul stuff."

When you spring your theme upon an audience, you are asking them to think. You dare not ask them to think too hard too soon. Remember that the way of the Persuader is to make people feel and let their feelings make them think. Trying to make a listener do a lot of thinking before he has much feeling for what you want him to think is about as effective as hitting a baseball with a styrofoam bat.

Some themes are *easier* and more *congenial* than others. There are times when your theme may be rather touchy, like the case of the sheriff back in Chapter 10 who was confronted by the angry mob determined to hang his prisoner. Actually the sheriff's theme was: "I'm going to see that this man gets a fair trial." But he didn't say it that way. He was a persuasive fellow. He was a Power Speaker. He took himself out of it by saying, ". . . the law says this man gets a fair shake." Nor did he start off by sounding his theme right away. He postponed it a bit until he had partially disarmed the mob with some light-hearted words that packed a serious thought and with some serious words that made the leaders of the mob identify with him in his problem. *He delayed his theme and he stated it indirectly.* Stated too soon and declared in its true form it would not have been congenial to this particular audience. Notice, however, that at the conclusion of his speech he popped his proposal boldly. And he spoke with Power.

DAVID AND GOLIATH AND A COUNTY SHERIFF

If your theme is: "Bodiddly Brown is a strong man with a courageous heart and a fine feeling for folks," you can state that theme when you first open your mouth because it is so *easy* to grasp and so *congenial* to hear. Then if you support your theme immediately with a David and Goliath story in which Bodiddly Brown saved Baby Boy Broderick from the wildcats you will cause your listeners to identify with your man, and if you conclude by shouting your proposal, "Vote for Bodiddly Brown for sheriff!" you and your big mouth will have probably elected a lawman.

BEWARE OF FUZZY POPPYCOCK

If your theme is: "Woman is God's loveliest flower, to be cultivated, nurtured, and protected by a stodgy gardener called man," you had better hold it from that female audience until you have established your sincerity, because that theme is fuzzy and abstract, and if sprung upon the girls at the beginning of your speech, it could come across like so much poppycock. The sound you would then hear floating up to the platform would be the death bell tolling the end of your proposal as some two-fisted tomboy springing to the podium would shout, "Up high to the sky with Women's Lib!"

THEMES THAT JAB LIKE A POINTED KNIFE

I know a football coach who got fired because he stood up at the Boosters Club banquet at the end of a disastrous season and started off his speech with this theme:

"This town will never have a winner."

That theme is easy to understand but it jabs a listener like a pointed knife. It is not *congenial*. The coach went on to support his theme with instance after instance that pictured very clearly why the town had never had a winning season in football. He picked on the players, he ridiculed their parents, he lambasted the school board, he criticized the Boosters Club, he hit them all squarely in the stomach with hard words. His idea was to make everybody in town so mad that they would all come rallying to the cause of football and help him hammer out a winning team. He ended his speech with this proposal:

"If you kids will stop smoking and drinking and carousing at night and if you parents will discipline these youngsters and if you boosters will get the fans out to the ball game and if you school board people will build us a new stadium, then *maybe* we can have a winning team. *Maybe!*"

That proposal is wishy-washy, but no matter—the listeners were not listening. They had made up their minds that the speaker was no longer their coach. And he wasn't.

Many a football coach the country over, finding himself in a similar position, has stood before nis players and his townspeople and painted a picture showing himself and them as a David facing Goliath, and has carefully explained some secret weapon that the community can develop that will enable them to kill their Goliath and become a champion. It has been done in football. It can be done in other things too.

Make your themes *easy;* there must be no sweat. Make them *congenial;* there must always be hope. If David could not lick Goliath, there would be no hope for survival, no way for recognition, no chance for romance, no reason for life. David has done it and he'll keep on doing it—over and over again.

12

JOTTING DOWN PICTURES THAT
COME WITH A POP

Now that you have sweat out the one little unforgettable sentence which will carry the thought of your entire speech, the hard work is over for awhile and the fun begins. So turn off your thinking-brain and let your feeling-brain take charge. Prop your theme up on the table in front of you and look at it. Drink it in. Soak it up. Let it become a living part of you. This is the nice little compact, eye-catching statement that you are going to nail to the ribs of your audience. It will become your battle cry as they go forth from the auditorium to tackle your proposal:

"Remember the Alamo!"
"Remember Pearl Harbor!"
"Remember Bodiddly Brown!"

What you need now is something to make your theme stick to their ribs. So place a long sheet of blank paper upon the table before you, take a sharp pencil into your hand, and gaze fondly upon the little unforgettable sentence. Don't try to think. Just relax and look. Let come what may.

Bang! Watch them arrive, the pictures that pop. Wow! Feel it flow, the energy that squirts. Every time a picture comes, jot it down on the long sheet of paper. Some of these pictures will be things you have done or seen somebody do. These personal things are the best. They are you. Some of them will be things you have read about or heard about. They are all good. They all made such an impression on you in the past that they became a living part of you when your feeling-brain grabbed them up and filed them away below the surface of your consciousness. Now here they come storming back to help you support your theme, to help you persuade an audience, to help you rise up and speak with *Power.*

HOGWASH AND PIG SLOP

There's only one way you can prevent these pictures from popping and that's for you to say:

"I can't do it, because I'm not creative."

Hogwash! Pig slop! Every prospective speaker throughout this big wide world is creative if he puts on a show of confidence so that his feeling-brain catches his act and feels that this man really believes in himself and actually intends making a speech using this particular theme. That pulsating little powerhouse will flood him with enough pictures for ten speeches.

Jot down everything that comes—*everything.* Some will seem silly. Put them down anyway. Don't judge these little things while they are hatching—even a newborn babe is an ugly little duckling at first sight. Some of these pictures will actually turn out to be silly, but had you failed to jot them down when they came, your feeling-brain would have backed off into a corner and begun to pout and there would have been no more pictures that day. You have to pamper your feeling-brain. So put down everything just as quickly and eagerly as you can. Use that energy. Write. Some of these things may turn out to be beautiful.

When bedtime comes, hit the sack. Sleep. Sometimes in the dead of night you may leap out of bed and rush to the Long Sheet and add a new item. Other times at break of day you may spring barefoot to the work table with a new shot. Whence came these pictures that popped in the night? Your thinking-brain was fast asleep, but your feeling-brain, which never sleeps, was eagerly at work popping pictures above the threshold. These night-time scenes were there for you to see, although you were not conscious of them until you awoke.

All this action will take place if you will first soak up the little unforgettable sentence that states the theme of your speech. The only way to halt the flood is to drive your feeling-brain into a dark corner of your cranium with the two silliest words in the English language: "I can't."

LETTING IDEAS COME AS THEY NATURALLY FLOW

If you are preparing a feature-length speech, a half-hour performance, let time go by, let the days pass, but set aside some moments each day or so to plop yourself down relaxed in front of your theme and give it a loving stare and add whatever items happen to come along that day. Do not pump anything yet. Just let everything come as it naturally flows.

One day out on the golf course, while you bask in the sunshine and suck in the fresh air and enjoy life in general, a new picture will pop, and it will be a dandy. Or it could happen while you are cranking in a big fish or playing poker at the club or bugging your orbs at a go-go girl. And this new picture will have absolutely nothing to do with what you were looking at or thinking about at the moment—completely irrelevant—but so appropriate to the theme propped up on your table back home. Once you have branded a theme on your brain, pictures to support it will come popping any second of the day, any moment of the night.

ROUSING YOUR BRAIN FROM ITS LANGUID LOUNGE

The time will finally come when the Long Sheet will be full top to bottom. Now, Mr. Speaker, it's time to stop having fun and go back to work. Maybe you took a trip to the library and read up on the subject of your speech. Perhaps you interviewed some dignitary for a little added information. Could be that the daily newspaper gave you a tip or two. Fine. These things are listed on the Long Sheet. But the best stuff in your speech will come from those personal experiences that live forever in your heart. The poem you copied at the library will pack a good punch in your conclusion or maybe you should use the quote you got from the dignitary. The statistics from the newspaper you can paint into a good moving picture that will add support to your theme.

Sweating time is here again. Time has come to rout your thinking-brain from its languid lounge. Your speech, whether five minutes long or forty-five, will have three parts: an *introduction*, a *development*, and a *conclusion*. In the introduction you will *sound your theme*, in the development you will *support that theme*, and in the conclusion you will *echo the theme*. Your whole speech will be about that one big idea. You will say absolutely nothing that will not advance that one unforgettable sentence.

Everything on your Long Sheet, be it silly or serious, weak or strong, deals with your theme because your theme gave birth to the entire litter. So stick with the list as you prepare your speech. If you stray from the list and stand up on speech night and tell a funny story just to be cute, you had better go hide in the depths of the woods because the mailman cometh bearing sad tidings: "The boys up at the front office want your union card!"

THREE CHEERS FOR THE LONG SHEET

Stick with your list. You may not use nearly all the items listed there. Great! That means you were really in there huffing and puffing. Just put this in your pipe and puff on it:

"Each little item on the Long Sheet made a solid contribution to my speech because each joined the chain reaction that kept ideas popping and energy squirting."

Three cheers for *the Long Sheet!*

13

FINDING A PICTURE TO SHOW OFF A THEME

Every Power Speaker does two things in the introduction of his speech: he sounds his theme, and he explains it. Sometimes he sounds it first and follows with the explanation. But at other times, when there is a good chance that an early statement of it would come across other than easy to understand or congenial to hear, he will delay the theme until he has prepared his listeners to receive it. While the proposal that he will spring at the end of his speech will be very specific, absolutely clear, and totally definite, the theme that he sounds in the beginning, no matter how clearly stated is still a generalization, an abstraction, a fuzzy thing, which asks his listeners to think. He knows that he dare not ask them to think before they want to think or else they will never think his thoughts. Remember, the winning way of the Power Speaker is to *make them feel and let their feelings make them think.*

TWO GIRLS WITH A WALLOP AND A MAN WITH A SOCK

Everything in this world is either *concrete* or *abstract*. You can explain a *concrete* thing simply by showing a picture of it. Hand me a photograph of a pretty girl standing beside a homely girl and I will know immediately what *beauty* is because *beauty* is *concrete* and I can see it. The contrast between the two girls packs a wallop. The pretty girl becomes beautiful and the homely girl becomes ugly. But stick under my nose a photograph of a courageous man standing alongside a coward and I cannot to save my life tell which is which because *courage* is *abstract* and I can't see it. Now then, Mr. Power Speaker, go sharpen up that silver tongue of yours and paint me a word picture of one of these two hombres in the photograph engaging in a conflict where the odds are against him but where he keeps on fighting anyway just because he feels that his cause is worth fighting for and living for if he can but dying for if he must, and I'll know exactly what *courage* is because I can *see what you mean when you make your picture move in a conflict that features an underdog against a top dog.* I not only *see* it but I *feel* it, and I want to take that underdog's part as he goes against that over-sized top dog. Your contrast packs a wallop. It makes me *identify*.

A *concrete* thing is easy to explain in a speech—just paint a word-picture of it. An *abstract* thing is also easy enough—just paint a word-picture of it *in action*.

THE GREATEST WORD IN OUR LANGUAGE

Themes are *abstract* at best. They cry out for help. Each begs for a supporting word-picture that will show a conflict which will explain with easy thinking just what the theme says.

Look again at this theme:

The one thing this poor old, uptight ball of earth needs
above all else is a thing called leadership, whose secret weapon
is a thing called persuasion.

Those words call for quite a bit of thinking. I did not dare
lead off with that theme as this book came rolling from the
press because the moment you read the first sentence you would
have slammed the volume shut and reached for something more
exciting, more thrilling, more romantic—something you could
see. So I opened the first chapter with a romantic story of leadership in action, in which Queen Elizabeth and her sea dogs
(Frobisher, Hawkins, and Drake) came up with a secret weapon
(seamanship) that gave them confidence and with a cause (England
forever!) that gave them courage. You *saw* without thinking too
hard what leadership *is* because you *saw* what leadership *does*.
Then I gave you a definition of leadership, which contains the
most important word in the English language, because I figured
you would now be ready to think a little harder:

Leadership is a force with a purpose that uses *persuasion*
as a tool to build morale as the stuff that explodes into action
and gets things done, and getting things done is the purpose—leadership gets things done.

Look at the word *persuasion*. You are gazing upon an abstract thing, but it is the most significant word in this book, and
the number one symbol in the English language. Why? Because persuasion is *Power:*

Our survival as a civilization depends on *persuasion* and
your survival in a competitive society depends on your ability
to *persuade—survival* spells *life*. Our recognition as a world
power and your recognition as a vibrant human being depends
on your ability to *persuade—recognition* spells *good life*. Our

romance in science and invention depends on *persuasion* and
your romance with exciting audiences depends on your ability
to *persuade*—*romance* spells *thrilling life*. *Persuasion* spells
good, thrilling life.

LETTING THE WORLD TAKE A LOOK

I devoted three early chapters to the David and Goliath
story because that story is the greatest illustration of persuasion
in action I have ever seen in my life, for it hangs something
up high for the whole world to see:

> As long as there lives on this earth a single human being
> willing to tackle odds and risk his life for a worthy cause,
> there shall be hope for all people everywhere, provided there
> come enough Power Speakers to paint a word-picture of that
> fighting man in action so that those who look and listen will
> *identify* with this lonely David, and, spurred by the *power of
> suggestion* will throw themselves with renewed hope against
> their own problems. All of which is another way of sounding
> my theme.

A BOLT FROM THE ETHER

So, Mr. Power Speaker, light up your pipe as you sit there
at your desk and screw your attention to the Long Sheet. Smoke
the list over carefully until you find a good picture that will
explain your theme. Then your introduction will be in the barn
ready for the market. If some evening, like a bolt from the ether,
some knuckle-headed toastmaster calls upon you to come forward
and say a few words, you can go bouncing to the microphone,
give the introduction of your half-hour address, state your proposal, and then sit down, and your remarks will register in the
minds of your listeners as a clever little three-minute talk given
off the cuff. Also, you probably will have earned yourself an

invitation to come back and be the main speaker some day soon.

TALKING THEM HOME FROM THE WILD BLUE YONDER

Suppose you happen to be a politician campaigning against the new trip to the moon, which will cost twenty billion dollars, and your proposal is:

Kill Lunar Bill 999.

What is your theme? It could be:

"There are better ways of spending twenty billion dollars
than by blasting a couple men off into the wild blue yonder."

In the development of your half-hour speech perhaps you support your theme by stating three better uses of the twenty billion. Possibly you have a strong address which just might kill Lunar Bill 999 if you can persuade enough listeners to persuade enough congressmen.

Then one night at the conclusion of your speech some long-haired microphone man from the TV station comes dashing up, sticks his instrument under your nose, and asks for a quick rundown for his viewing audience, an audience perhaps of millions. Here is a chance that's golden, Mr. Speaker. But what can you do in three minutes? *You can do plenty:*

"There are better ways of spending twenty billion dollars
than by blasting a couple men off into the wild blue yonder."

This is your theme. It's easy to understand. It's already congenial enough to large hordes of the population, and not uncongenial to many others who go about shrugging their shoulders at moon trips but who can be persuaded to join your cause. So you can state your theme, follow with the three main points

in your development, and pop your proposal, and there probably
would be much nodding-of-the-head by your listeners. But would
they spring into action against the moon trip? You have appealed
to their thinking-brains with the logic of your entire speech,
but you have done little to their feeling-brains.

Personally I would do it this way: I would state the theme,
paint a picture of it, and then pop the proposal, not even touching
on the development, the three supporting points—not in three
minutes. Here's why: I don't know how much money twenty
billion dollars is. Do you? I don't even know how much one
billion dollars is. It sounds like a lot of lucre. But I cannot
see it. I cannot *feel* it. I cannot *appreciate* it. All because I
do not get the picture.

But I wish it were possible to snap a photograph of that
vast audience when you stick your long finger into the camera
and follow your theme with a word picture like this:

> "Sending a man to the moon will require a bridge of ten-
> dollar bills that will stretch end to end from the earth off into
> space until the last ten-spot touches the horns of the moon
> 240,000 miles away. Look here, friend: those precious ten-spots
> stretching forth out there in the bright sunshine are *yours*. Look
> at the lovely things fluttering in the breeze. Now watch them
> go up in smoke—every one of them. That's your money, friend,
> burnt to a crisp! Would you like to rescue that hard-earned
> money? You can do it: write your congressman—kill Lunar
> Bill 999!"

THE ENTIRE SPEECH IN THE SHELL OF A NUT

The introductions of feature-length speeches when coupled
with the proposals from the conclusions become effective little
compact talks all by themselves. Each of them can live alone
and survive because each contains the theme of the main address

with a moving picture of that theme which, when the speaker attaches his proposal, challenges the audience with a call to action. He hits their total-brain, both the thinking part and the feeling part.

Thus an introduction, which states the problem mentally and explains it emotionally, can, by borrowing the proposal, tell the listener what to do about the problem. A good introduction with proposal added is really the whole speech in the shell of a nut. So, Mr. Persuader, work out introductions that are eye-pleasing and ear-catching so you can be ready to speak long or short.

Get ready now to plunge into the second part of a Power Speech, the *development* of the theme, where if we exercise a little care we can make those introductions lead into something soul-searing and enable ourselves to be *Powerfully persuasive*.

14

SUPPORTING YOUR THEME WITH ONE SINGLE SHOT

Consider again the action you want from your audience at the conclusion of your speech. Look once more at the theme propped up on your desk that you hope will spur your people to act. Now take the Long Sheet into your hand and prepare to use your thinking-brain. The big chore is at hand: how best to support the theme so that *it becomes a battle cry for action.*

You could come to the podium rated the world's foremost genius and proceed to hit your audience with the greatest flow of logic that ever fell on human ears as you explain why they should rush forth and get going on your proposal. But if logic is all you give them, the intellectuals in the group will go strolling forth from the auditorium arm in arm discussing your speech and nodding their heads and admiring the thinking-brain of the speaker. They will spend a little time during the days that lie ahead pouring over your proposal with their own thinking-brains. But pouring may be all that they will ever do about it.

There will be some there that evening, less endowed mentally than the intellectuals, who will come away slow-footed and weary, thinking about nothing in particular, while others will come away big-eyed and jolly because some natural-born leader in their section during your speech whispered the news about Mike Shagnasty and Susie McGoosie. These frolicking fellows don't even remember what you said. They were tuned in on a different wave length, seeing things and feeling things you did not make them see and feel because you were holding forth with nothing but good sound logic. Action you wanted but no action you got. You failed as a Persuader. How silly! Anybody can persuade somebody. Certainly you must use logic because logic will justify the action to come, but how do you get the action to come?

GETTING THE ACTION TO COME

Gaze upon the Long Sheet. Here you have the answer. You have stories here, some long, some short, some medium-size, some concerning you, some about other people, some true, some fancied. You have quotations here, poems and famous sayings by famous people; you have statistics here, which in picture form can be made to sparkle and shine; you have little sub-themes here, small bits of logic that support your main theme—you have here everything you need to drive your theme into the hearts of your listeners and get the action you want.

You cannot possibly in a half-hour use all the items you have listed on the Long Sheet. You may not use half of them, or even one-tenth. You may have enough material here to write a book. But every single item you have written down, whether you use it in your speech or not, will play its part because each was spawned by your theme, and together they add up to one big solid support that will bolster your confidence in that theme and crank up your feeling for it—confidence *in* it and feeling *for* it—both of which, when you finally mount the platform to speak your piece, will bring you on stage with *the authoritative manner of a man taking charge.*

THE SINGLE SHOT AND THE SCATTER GUN

There are only two methods of developing any theme, the Single Shot and the Scatter Gun. In the Single-Shot Method you will pick from the Long Sheet a David and Goliath story in which some famous person, living or dead, started from humble beginnings and by using a particular skill that he had worked on until he had gotten good at it and thrilled with it rose up against great odds and landed on top of the heap. This one story can form the bulk of your speech. The audience will identify with your David. They will become your David in their hearts. They will want to take his place. So you echo your theme in the conclusion and issue your challenge and send them scurrying forth to meet their own particular Goliath.

LITTLE BOY BE GOOD

Does the following scene look familiar to you?

You want your little son Johnny to be a good boy so that he will grow up to become a good man. One thing you most certainly do not do—you do not set him on your lap, stroke his long, unshorn locks, and say to him:
"*Johnny, be good.*"
The poor little fellow won't have the slightest idea what you're talking about. What is *good? Good* is *abstract.*

However if you tell him a story about somebody doing a *good* job so that he identifies with this person and wants to be like him, then you are wielding the greatest of all secret weapons for winning the battle with youngsters, *identification* and *suggestion*—the watchdogs of *persuasion*.

On other days the little guy will come crawling back to your lap and he will say:

"Daddy, tell me a story."

Again he wants a single shot from you. Once more he yearns to identify with some young David, to feel the thrill of David's challenge and the warmth of recognition that follows David's success and the sense of security that comes with David's survival: *romance, recognition, survival*—these three —remember?

So you talk and he *identifies*. Then he jumps off your lap and goes springing into the great out-of-doors sounding a man-size battle cry:

"Fight! Win! Achieve!"

Across the way some hippie kid replies with a moaning wail:

"Peace, love, joy."

That hippie lad just might become your youngster's Goliath. If so, you have prepared your boy well for the conflict. You did it with the Single-Shot Method—often repeated—*one good story to support one good theme to build one good boy.*

PODIUM POUNDING CHAMP

Ministers make frequent use of the Single-Shot Method because they must mount the pulpit every Sunday morning with a brand new sermon, and this method is ideal because it is easy.

Did you ever hear Billy Graham preach a sermon? There's a Great Persuader, that man Graham, a Power Speaker of the first water. I made up my mind some time ago, after thirty-eight years of barn-storming about the country, to give up podium pounding and write more books, but I heard Billy Graham one night in Kentucky and the Great Persuader sent me bubbling southward with a new determination. I am still holding forth in the knife-and-fork league.

Here is a brief rundown on a typical Graham lecture: He recites a few lively verses from the Bible; he abstracts a theme from that quotation; he paints an oral picture of the theme so you can see what he is talking about; then he develops that theme with one long Bible story which he intersperses now and then with little modern-day stories—things he has read in the newspapers (he subscribes to many newspapers) or things he has seen on television—all of which keep drawing his Bible story up to the present moment, while again and again during this development he repeats his theme until it builds up into a thrilling refrain. Finally he concludes his lecture by challenging his audience to come to the altar and stand before him while he prays their souls into Heaven, and, friend, I defy you to hear this man and not accept his proposal. How can you turn down *everlasting survival, permanent recognition, and eternal romance?*

Billy Graham makes masterful use of the Single-Shot Method by tossing into his single narrative little tid-bits of fact or fancy, story, quotation, statistic and pieces of experience that make his one big story come booming home to his listeners.

If you occupy a position where time after time you have to get up and face virtually the same audience, then the Single-Shot Method of supporting a theme is just the thing for you.

15

SPREADING YOUR THEME
WITH A SCATTER GUN

David killed Goliath with a single shot, but he held several other stones in his left hand just in case he missed. Had a third stone been necessary this last shot would have been critical because by that time Goliath would have closed in swinging his thirty-pound sword.

The Scatter-Gun Method of supporting a theme means taking several shots to bring your audience to its knees. The numeral *three* seems to be the most critical number in any language. The third strike means you're out; the third time you go under means you're drowned; the third part of your speech means you are concluding and with that conclusion you have won or you have lost.

BRINGING GOLIATH DOWN WITH SEX

So with the Scatter-Gun Method you divide your development into three sections. You can head these divisions with various names: three adverbs like *physically, mentally,* and *spiritually;* or three nouns like *past, present,* and *future;* or three questions like *what, why,* and *how;* or three classifications like *big-bosomed blondes, swivel-hipped brunettes,* and *over-sexed redheads;* or any other way you choose, *but* the third section must be the most exciting part of your speech because this is your critical moment. This is the stone that must kill Goliath. If you are developing your theme *physically, mentally,* and *spiritually,* the spiritual point must *draw them to the altar.* If you are developing it with *past, present,* and *future,* the big emphasis is not on "where you have been or where you are right now but *where you are going."* If you are supporting your theme with the three questions, *what, why,* and *how,* you tell them *what* should be done, *why* it should be done, and then show them why it has never been done: nobody knew *how—so you show them how.* If you are expounding on man's greatest weakness—*big-bosomed blondes, swivel-hipped brunettes,* and *over-sexed redheads*—you save those redheads until last because those pulsating creatures can bring Goliath down without firing a shot.

ENDING STRONG WITH THE TEAR-JERKER LAST

If you plan to use three short stories to support your theme, Mister, beware! Too much of the same kind of material to push the same point begins to lose its vigor. Similar stories do indeed show the truth of your theme, but the truth can grow weary with too much repetition, when actually it should be getting more and more dynamic, more reassuring, more thrilling as you go. Similar things *type* each other. But contrasting things *emphasize*. Do you recall the photograph of the pretty girl who became beautiful because she stood beside a homely girl who became ugly? Contrast packs a wallop.

So if you plan to use three short stories in your development, pick a couple that show the beautiful results of putting your theme into action and a third that pictures the ugly state of affairs when the opposite is true, *and throw the tear-jerker in last.* You will not be winding up your talk on a negative note because you will then come on strong with your conclusion in which you will echo your theme and pop your proposal, *which is very positive!*

Another way of using the Scatter-Gun Method is by dividing your theme into three sub-themes and supporting each of these points with short-short stories or dramatic statistics or startling facts or bits of logic or anything, fact or fancy, that will help show the truth of the point you are making. All this supporting material you can find on the Long Sheet that your creative feeling-brain helped you compile during the picture-popping days of your early preparation.

WHEN THE LISTENERS GROW WEARY

The Scatter-Gun Method requires more sweat than the Single-Shot but it prepares a very flexible program. Some night when the hour grows late and the audience weary and you want to shorten your speech, you can throw out section number one or number two or both and use pulsating section number three as a single shot. If the toastmaster waits until midnight to call your creaking bones to the microphone, you can even throw out number three and use the oral picture back in your introduction as a single shot to give the sleepy-eyed audience a quickie before sending them home to bed.

PROPOSAL PLUS THEME PLUS PICTURE THAT MOVES

Suppose you are to address the local Rotary Club at its weekly luncheon where you will have only about twenty minutes to speak your piece. Rotarians like to be entertained during these relaxed moments away from the grunts and groans of the daily grind. So you plan to entertain them with some light-hearted words but you also mean to stick to their ribs a serious message that will come oozing out of your frivolous phrases. Let's try something like this:

Your proposal: To give these Rotarians a few chuckles, a quicker circulation of the blood, and a faster footstep back to the office.

Your theme: "Every successful Rotarian fires a Triple-Shot Scatter Gun."

Your theme in action: Once upon a time down along the muddy waters of the Rio Grande a bunch of the boys were whooping it up in a roadside tavern called The Fish Hook. They called this watering trough The Fish Hook because it was located down at the end of the line.

It was Saturday night, payday on the range, and quite a few big-eyed boys had ridden in for a bit of fun and frivolity at The Fish Hook Tavern. The place was crowded. Men stood belly-up-to-the-bar elbow to elbow drinking a cactus brew known as Mexican Red-eye. Others sat crowding the gaming tables all about the big room, while in amongst the boys moved the girls, the swivel-hipped señoritas, making eyes at the fellows.

Now some of these guys were innocent country boys, not even dry behind the ears yet and with their mother's last kiss still fresh on their lips, being lured by the painted women in The Fish Hook Tavern.

Suddenly amidst all this merriment the swinging doors of The Fish Hook swung violently inward and a Young Man from the Mountains leaped into the room, jumped to the top of the bar, and fired a shot into the ceiling.

"That's *one!*" he roared.

Then he fired a shot into the wall on his left.

"That's *two!*" he cried.

He followed with a bullet into the wall on his right.

"That's *three!*"

Then he poured a slug into the wall across the room.

"That's *four!*"

Finally he pumped a hot bullet into a crowded poker table in the middle of the room.

"That's *five!* That leaves only one shot more. Who wants the last shot. I'll tell you who gets it: *Whoever is last when I say go!*"

He waved his weapon toward the opposite side of the room.

"To the wall!" he roared. "Face the boards. Press your noses upon the planks. And wait for me. *On your marks, get set, go!*"

They went, every mother's son of them, and every father's daughter. They leaped to the wall in one solid mass. They faced the boards. They pressed their noses upon the planks. They waited.

Then the Young Man from the Mountains jumped down from the bar and strode across the room unbuttoning his shirt as he went. Starting at the end of the line to his left he removed the first man's billfold and stuffed it into the bosom of his unbuttoned shirt. Down the line he moved gathering billfolds from the men and slapping the señoritas on the rump with the back of his hand.

"That's one you owe me, Toots," he said to each señorita as he passed. He was proceeding nicely now and nearing the end of the line.

Suddenly the swinging doors of The Fish Hook swung inward once more, not so violently this time, rather casually in fact, and an Old Man of the Desert strolled into the place, ambled across to the bar, and smote the planks with a gnarled fist.

"Mr. Bartender," he said, "wherever you are, give me a hamburger with onions and a glass of cool, clear water."

The bartender was at the wall, facing the boards, nose on the planks. He didn't move.

The Young Man from the Mountains looked at the Old Man of the Desert. The Young Man's chin fell upon his chest, his tongue flopped out, his eyes bugged forth, his ears flapped his breath came in hot pants. Then getting a firm hold on himself he strode angrily across the room and shoved several inches of his pistol barrel into the midregion of the Old Man of the Desert.

"Old Man," he said, "you get your quaking old fingers up real high or I'll prosecute you—I'll prosecute you to the fullest extent of this old .44 calibre thunderball!"

Slowly the Old Man of the Desert raised his hands and *slowly* he looked into the eyes of the Young Man from the Mountains and *slowly* he lowered his gaze upon the white knuckle of the trigger finger and the straining thumb that held back the cocked hammer of the big six-shot pistol. *Slowly* the Old Man raised his eyes until they met once again the angry orbs of the Young Man.

*Quickly—quickly—quickly—*like the flashing jump of a lightning bolt the long lean left arm of the Old Man of the Desert leaped downward and the left hand smacked upon the pistol chamber and the middle finger of that left hand fell into the gap between the cocked hammer and the firing pin.

Then came three quick sounds that were so similar you almost have to spell them the same way:

Thup! That was the sound made as the *leaping* hammer of the big pistol ground into the middle finger of the Old Man of the Desert.

Thop! That was the sound made as the *leaping* right fist of the Old Man of the Desert smashed against the jaw of the Young Man from the Mountains causing the gunman to turn a *leaping* somersault backwards that carried him into the further-most corner of The Fish Hook Tavern.

Thap! That was the sound made as the Old Man of the Desert turned to the bar and smote the planks with the bruised fist that had *leaped*.

"Mr. Bartender," he said, "wherever you are, give me a hamburger with onions and a glass of cool, clear water."

The bartender came running. The patrons of The Fish Hook Tavern pounced upon the Young Man from the Mountains. They ripped the shirt off his back. Billfolds flew in all directions. Men scampered about madly like a bunch of scalded cats. When everybody had recovered his hard-earned lucre, they all gathered around the Old Man of the Desert.

"Old Man," they said, "how'd you do it, hmn, how'd you do it, hmn, how'd you do it?"

The Old Man of the Desert said never a word. Slowly he munched upon his hamburger with onions. Slowly he sipped his glass of cool, clear water. Finally he wiped his mouth on the back of a gnarled fist and turned to his audience.

"Ladies and gentlemen," he said, "have you a question at this time?"

"Yes, Old Man of the Desert, how'd you do it, hmn, how'd you do it, hmn, how'd you do it?"

"Ladies and gentlemen, I am an Old Man of the Desert. I have lived a long life. I have done many things. I have learned very much. There have been times when I have holed up for the winter in some far-off cave and almost starved to death for want of a hamburger with onions. There have been other times when I have lain out on the hot dusty desert with my tongue sticking out of my mouth like a boiled sweet potato dying for want of a drink of cool, clear water. And there have been times when I have fallen to the earth before some gunman's hot lead and lain there helplessly watching my heart's blood slaking the thirsty sod.

"I am an Old Man of the Desert. I have lived a long life. I have done many things. I have learned very much. But the most valuable lesson I have learned during my entire life is the secret of that little skill you saw me demonstrate here tonight."

"Old Man of the Desert, how'd you do it, hmn, how'd you do it, hmn, how'd you do it?"

"Ladies and gentlemen, I'm going to give you my secret but first I want you to do a little something for me. I want you to take this old nine-gallon hat—this used to be a ten-gallon hat but the Ration Board cut me down a gallon during the Indian War—I want you to pass this old nine-gallon hat around amongst you. I want each of you men to dig deep into his pants. I want each of you ladies to reach tenderly into her bosom. I want everybody here to come up with lots of that nice, soft, green stuff that buys groceries. I do not want too many aces—let there be plenty of fivers and some ten-shuns and even a few twenty-dollar williams. Fill this old nine-gallon hat with legal tender and I'll give you my life-long secret."

In just a few feverish moments the battered old hat was filled to the brim and brought overflowing to the Old Man of the Desert. Pulling the stuffed head-piece down hard upon his balding dome the Old Man faced his audience.

"Ladies and Gentlemen, listen carefully. Here is my secret:

Number One: *I thought I could do it.*
Number Two: *I had the guts to try it.*
Number Three: *I had a cause worth fighting for—my fellow man.*"

Slowly but very deliberately the Old Man pushed through the astounded crowd, which parted before him like the Red Sea before Moses, and shoved through the swinging doors. He disappeared into the blackness of the night. The Old Man of the Desert was gone.

Some long-haired kook from the Upper Ravines jumped to the top of the bar.

"By the gee-jumping John Henry." he roared, "we've been robbed again! The only difference between the Young Man from the Mountains and the Old Man of the Desert is the Young Man used a gun and the Old Man used his mouth! Let's go after him and hang him to the highest tree in Calhoun County!"

"Hold it!" yelled the bartender as he rapped the audience to order by pounding his pistol butt upon the bar. "That Old Man was absolutely honest. He made a deal with us. He sold us the Triple-Shot Scatter Gun called Confidence, Courage, and Cause—these three—and we got our money's worth. All his life he practiced on a skill until he got so good at it that he could work wonders using it the way he used it here tonight. We just bought ourselves the Triple-Shot Scatter Gun and we got our money's worth. The drinks are on the house."

That bartender happened to be a charter member of the Noble Knights of Power Speaking.

QUICKER BLOOD AND FASTER FEET

You have just completed your introduction. You have sounded your theme and painted a picture of it in action. Remember, a good introduction makes a nice little compact speech all by itself, so if the building suddenly catches fire, you can yell after those fleeing Rotarians as they go diving out the windows:

> "Every successful Rotarian fires the Triple-Shot Scatter Gun called Confidence, Courage, and Cause."

Your speech is over. All you gave them was your introduction plus your conclusion. Your proposal, which you never mentioned, is being acted upon, especially the quicker circulation of the blood and the faster footsteps back to the office.

HOW TO SPRAY WORDS WITH A TRIPLE SHOT

However, if the building has not caught fire, you can go on with the development of your theme using the Scatter-Gun Method:

> Point Number One: Every time a Rotarian steps into his office he locks horns with the problems of the day. If he licks those problems he comes away from his office with his head up and a gleam in his eye.

"Honey," he says to his wife, "I put in a good day and made a good dollar."

A powerful positive punch begins to pound down deep inside that Rotarian. Day after day he meets problems and licks those problems and goes springing from his office with that powerful positive punch pounding harder than ever down deep inside him:

"Yet another day and yet another dollar."

The name of that powerful positive punch? It's a thing called *confidence*. Confidence that he learned in a business or professional office practicing a skill until he got so good at it and so thrilled with it that he wanted to use it outside his office for a greater cause. So he became a Rotarian, because a Rotarian uses his skill to render a service to his community and to his country and to his world.

Point Number Two: Every time a Rotarian steps into his office and locks horns with the problems of the day and those problems knock him down, he has to get back on his feet and throw himself back into the fight. He can't just lie there. His secretary wants him up. His wife wants him up. His associates want him up.

"Get up, fellow, get up! Get up, fellow, get up!"

So he gets up and throws himself back into the fight, and gets a little sand in his craw. Thousands of times during a long career a Rotarian gets knocked down, and thousands of times he gets back on his feet, and thousands of times he throws himself back into the fight and each time he gets a little sand in his craw. That's a lot of sand in that fellow's craw. The name of that sand in the craw? It's a thing called *courage*. Courage that he learned locking horns with the problems of the day and getting knocked down but always getting up and throwing himself back into the fight:

"These are great days and these are great dollars."

Point Number Three: Every time a group of Rotarians get together to decide what they can do to make life better and more thrilling for their community and their country and their world they shake hands and pledge themselves each to the other to go all out, to use every ounce of their energy and every spark of their spirit, to employ all their skill as business men and professional people to make their plan work. The name of that shaking of hands and pledging of hearts? It's a thing called "fighting for a cause that's worth fighting for." What makes their cause worth fighting for? They are fighting to bring a better, more thrilling life to their fellow man:

"These are the best days and these are the best ways to spend the best dollars."

Conclusion: "Every successful Rotarian fires a Triple-Shot Scatter Gun called Confidence, Courage, and Cause—these three—so, gentlemen, congratulations to all of you and let's get on with our work."

Such is the flexibility of the Scatter-Gun Method of developing a theme. It covers a wide panorama of possibilities. It challenges a speaker to add the strength of his thinking-brain to the creative fire-power of his feeling-brain. That challenge says:

"Let's *organize*, Man!"

16

POPPING YOUR PROPOSAL

Winston Churchill shook his fist at 2000 German bombers screaming overhead and delivered the greatest conclusion any speech has ever known:

> We shall not flag or fail. We shall go on to the end. We shall fight in France, we shall fight on the seas and oceans, we shall fight with growing confidence and with growing strength in the air, we shall defend our island, whatever the cost may be, we shall fight on the beaches, we shall fight on the landing grounds, we shall fight in the fields and in the streets, we shall fight in the hills; we shall never surrender.

Or as the old football coach would say:

> "Let's go! Let's fight! Let's win!"

SENDING THE AUDIENCE SOARING

Even though you have developed your theme to its highest peak when you fire your critical shot in the main body of your speech, you are not yet home free. You must send those listeners soaring away. You need to blast them off the launching pad. You have to pop your proposal—I mean really make it crack.

Physics professors, appealing purely to the thinking-brains of their students, conclude their lectures with a summary of the important points they have been developing. Not so, a Power Speaker. He has no need to summarize. The moving picture he painted in his introduction to show his theme in action and the pictures he portrayed as he developed that theme in the main body of his speech have all been snatched by the feeling-brains of his listeners and hauled away safely to their memory galleries. Their adrenalin flows. They bristle with morale. All they need now is for the starting gun to sound—for the proposal to pop.

LIGHTING THE WAY WITH A VERBAL TORCH

Did you ever read William Jennings Bryan's famous "Cross of Gold" conclusion? Perhaps you hold nothing against the gold standard—I don't—but does not this fellow make you want to roll up your sleeves and do battle for whatever he proposes. Here's the way he said it:

> If they dare come at us with the gold standard, we will fight them to the uttermost! We will answer their demands by saying to them: You shall not press down upon the brow of labor this crown of thorns; *you shall not crucify mankind upon a cross of gold!*

Our man Lincoln was certainly no slouch at concluding a speech. Honest Abe knew how to make you identify with him and with the proposal he was suggesting:

> With malice toward none, with charity for all . . . let us strive on to finish the work we are in: to bind up the nation's wounds, to care for him who fought the battle . . . to do all we can to achieve a just and lasting peace among ourselves and with all nations.

Winston Churchill was carrying a torch for *survival*. So was William Jennings Bryan. So was Abraham Lincoln. In your proposal you may be appealing to the same basic cause, or you may be emphasizing *recognition*, or even *romance*, or any combination of these three basic causes for action.

But suppose you are presenting a proposal that the audience wants done but one that they don't think they can handle. They lack confidence. Your emphasis now is on their secret weapon. Everybody has a secret weapon, but people without confidence don't know what it is. Your secret weapon is your knowledge of how to motivate people. So your job here is to point out to your audience exactly what their secret weapon is, to let them *see* it, to make them *feel* it.

GOING TO HEAVEN WITH A ROYAL FLUSH

Do you recall the big cotton-farming preacher back in Chapter 2 whose sermon on David and Goliath put the theme of this book into action? Here's how that rawbone man of God worked on a listener's confidence:

> One fine Sunday morning the whole countryside gathered on the banks of Rawhide River to watch Big Preacher Parkins baptize a group of new converts.

Old Ebeneezer Collins was first to be baptized. Ebeneezer was a sinner from way back, but he had a wife who was a saintly woman and a tireless worker for the church. She never gave up on anybody.

"As long as the body is warm, there is hope for the soul," she would say.

Finally after all these many years she had prevailed upon old Ebeneezer to come to the River and get his soul purified. Today he was here, white shirt and tie and blue serge suit—his very best going-to-meetin' clothes.

The preacher took Ebeneezer by the arm and together they waded out toward deeper water. When they were waist deep, slowly there came floating forth from one of Ebeneezer's side pockets the Ten of Spades, and from another pocket came the Jack. The crowd snickered. The preacher led his convert onward.

When the water was belly deep, gently from one of Ebeneezer's vest pockets floated the Queen of Spades and from another came the King. The crowd laughed. The preacher guided his convert doggedly onward.

When they were armpit deep, lazily from Ebeneezer's inside coat pocket floated the Ace of Spades. The crowd roared. The preacher stopped. The water was deep enough.

"Hold it, Parson!" screamed Mrs. Ebeneezer Collins, the saintly woman who never gave up on anybody. "Bring Ebeneezer back. Bring him back! He's lost, *lost,* LOST—LOST I tell you!"

The saintly woman had given up.

"Sister Collins," said Preacher Parkins, *"how in the hell can he be lost with a hand like that!"*

THE TWO THUNDERBOLTS OF POWER SPEAKING

Every audience has good cards in its pockets. Your job and mine is to float those cards out upon open waters so all can see and behold their secret weapon. That weapon could be any one of many things: their good education, their business skill, their public spirit, their professional acumen, their teamwork, their zest for the good life, or it could be nothing more than a great big collective chestful of courage that any human being can come up with when his cause is right.

Like all good persuasive speakers, Patrick Henry cranked up his countrymen's courage by using the two thunderbolts of Power Speaking: *identification* and *suggestion*.

> Is life so dear or peace so sweet as to be purchased at the price of chains and slavery? Forbid it Almighty God! I know not what course others may take but *as for me, give me liberty or give me death!*

Here was David daring to face Goliath. Here was listener identification melting a big audience into one intrepid young David. Here was the power of psychological suggestion drawing together an entire wilderness of assorted human beings, drawing them with the world's greatest drawing cards: *survival, recognition, romance* —these three—which could lead them all to a *better, more thrilling life*—IF David killed Goliath!

The IF is BIG! So just before he spoke his flaming words to kindle his countrymen's courage, Patrick Henry said something to bolster their confidence:

> They tell us we are weak—unable to cope with an adversary so strong. Sir, we are not weak! . . . Three million people armed in the holy cause of liberty . . . are invincible from any force our enemy can send against us. Besides we shall not fight our battles alone. There is a just God who will raise up friends for us . . . The war is inevitable—let it come! I repeat, sir, let it come!

So Patrick Henry and his people went forth to face Goliath, but not until they had practiced a few military skills that they got so good at and so thrilled with that they were able to use them to carve out a new civilization in the North American wilderness.

SOUND AND ECHO

The conclusion of your speech will resemble the introduction. The two will match each other. In the introduction you sounded a theme. In the conclusion you will echo that sound by restating the theme word for word. In the introduction you explained your theme with a picture that put the theme into action. In the conclusion you will revitalize the explanation with another moving picture that will squeeze off the trigger. Here is a great spot for a thrilling poem. Have you listed one on the Long Sheet? If so, memorize it—learn it by heart—so you can look your audience in the eye and deliver your message with your whole body talking. Rhythm and rhyme that carry a good picture can stir a listener's feeling-brain to the point of explosion, and Mr. Power Speaker, explosion is exactly what you want. So recite that poem and hurl that challenge and get out of the way and watch the walls go tumbling down.

I have used quite a number of poems back over the years, but the one that never fails to bring a request for a printed copy is the following anonymous lyric done in ballad stanza:

> Life is a game with a glorious prize
> If we can only play it right.
> It is give and take, build and break,
> And sometimes it ends in a fight.
> But he surely wins who honestly tries
> Regardless of wealth or fame.
> He can never despair who plays it fair—
> Say, Man! How are *you* playing the game?
>
> Do you wilt and whine if you fail to win
> In a manner you think your due?
> Do you sneer at the man in case that he can,

And does, do better than you?
Or do you take your rebuffs with a knowing grin
And do you laugh though you pull up lame?
Does your faith hold true when the whole world's blue?
Say, Man! How are you *playing* the game?

Well, get into the think of it, friend,
Whatever your cherished goal.
Brace up your will 'til your pulses thrill
And you dare to your very soul.
Do something more than make a noise—
Let your purpose leap into flame,
As you plunge with a cry, "I shall do or die!"
Then, Man! you'll be *playing* the game!

That poem is my favorite. It not only echoes my pet theme, but it also pops my pet proposal: "Let's go! Let's fight! Let's win!"

17

THE POWER WAY TO MASTER A SPEECH

Congratulations! You have finally put a persuasive speech upon the drawing board. You did it by proceeding according to the following work-sheet:

Proposal

I want my audience to do *this* particular thing (write it down).

Introduction

I   I will sound my theme in *these* words. (Write it down exactly the way you plan to say it.)
    A. Putting my entire speech into one unforgettable sentence.
    B. And making my theme *easy* to understand and *congenial* to hear.

II.   I will put my theme into action with *this* particular moving picture. (Indicate the picture.)
  A. Showing exactly what I mean by my theme.
  B. And using fact or fancy, anything from the Long Sheet that will explain the theme.

Development

I.   If I use the Single-Shot Method I will do the following:
  A. Paint a picture of *this* particular conflict featuring *this* particular underdog against *this* awesome opponent. (Phrase the situation in one statement.)
  B. Give the underdog *this* particular secret weapon that he has practiced on until he has gained confidence in its use. (Name the weapon.)
  C. Arouse the underdog's courage by appealing to his basic sense of survival, recognition, or romance or any combination thereof. (List the appeals to be used.)
  D. Throw him against his awesome opponent and let him win. (Put his victory into one compact statement.)
  E. Show the audience how they are in the same boat as my underdog. (Write only one sentence.)
  F. Point out their own secret weapon. (Name it.)
  G. Appeal to the three basic causes of all motivated action: survival, recognition, romance. (List the causes to which you plan to appeal.)
II.   If I employ the Scatter-Gun Method I will proceed as follows:
  A. Divide the development of my theme into *these* three particular categories. (List the categories but leave room enough to mention the illustrations.)
  B. Support each category as if it were my main theme with *these* particular details. (List the details.)

Conclusion

I. I will echo my theme exactly as I sounded it in the introduction. (Write it down again—brand it on your brain.)

II. I will revitalize that sound with *this* particular story or poem or flaming statistic or startling fact. (Show the illustration to be used.)

III. Finally I will pop my proposal. (Write it down exactly the way you plan to say it— drive it into your heart.)

HOW TO SPEAK AND SAVE YOUR LIFE

The moment you finish filling in the work-sheet, the hard job is over. The thinking-brain can go take a rest. Your ideas are down on paper. The skeleton of your speech lies before you. This is your working outline. And that is all the writing you will do on this speech. You absolutely *will not write out this speech word for word* while you are making it up—just the outline—because the Noble Knights of Power Speaking *hate to see you die so young!*

Later when you have mastered the speech, you can write it out for the newspaper boys or your book editor or your adoring progeny, but just try writing it down as you make it up and, Noble Knight—you will never know labor more grueling and grinding.

Your mind can throw words at you sixteen times as fast as you can put them down on paper. Every time you write one word fifteen more will come crowding and pushing. Your nervous fingers will turn to stone. It's a good way to go stark raving mad!

If you try to write out your speech word for word as you make it up, you will be putting words together the way writers write them, not the way speakers speak them. Your speech will be nothing more than a bunch of written words that you will have to recite from memory or read to your audience—God forbid—and the whole thing will come off like an essay, which is exactly what it will be, an essay being recited or read. How utterly dreary! You and I have got to stand up and look our people in the eye and speak *to* them, not recite *at* them, nor read *for* them.

HOW THE WORLD'S GREATEST SPEAKER LEARNED HIS LESSON

The first time Winston Churchill got up to address Parliament, his mind went blank and his eyes popped wide and he mumbled a few gurgling sounds and sat down embarrassed to the depths of his great soul because his mind had forgotten everything! He thought his career as a statesman had come to an end before it had scarcely started. *He had memorized his speech word for word.*

When H. V. Kaltenborn, one-time dean of American newscasters, was a college student, he took part in a speech contest. He selected a short story entitled "Gentleman, the King" as his presentation. He memorized the story word for word. The day he got up to speak he mounted a four foot platform, looked out at his big-eyed, Harvard classmates and froze in his boots. His mind took a sudden vacation. He staggered back a couple steps, falling off the platform, and his classmates rolled out of their seats with laughter. Kaltenborn got mad. He jumped back upon the platform. He lit into that startled audience with flailing arms and pounding fists and told his story the way he saw the pictures moving in his mind's eye. The judges awarded him first prize in the contest.

MAKING YOUR SPEECH A SURE-FIRE THING

If you memorize your speech word for word, you will go to the podium and start looking for those words on the television screen of your mind. There will be entirely too many fuzzy little symbols. They will appear a jumbled mess. Yet you may still save the day by looking for pictures. If pictures come they will draw words into your mouth like a magnet drawing iron filings.

There's only one sure way to master a speech: Look at your outline and see the pictures and start talking your speech to yourself. Do you know where all those words are coming from? From your memory storehouse. Do you know who is in charge of your memory storehouse? Your feeling-brain, which cannot think but certainly can see and loves to watch television. Remember, also, that the feeling-brain has a hotline that leads right straight to the emotions.

So gaze upon that outline and see the pictures you have listed there, and your feeling-brain will send a quick message down to the emotions: "Sock it to 'em, knock 'em down, hit!" From out of your depths will come a burst of energy squirting and a surge of words flowing.

Therefore, lay that pencil down, Man, and keep looking at your work-sheet and keep talking to yourself. When you finish your introduction, go back and do it two more times. Then go to the development. Speak it through three times. Now on to the conclusion. Say it three times.

Finally start at the beginning and go through the entire speech—three times. That's enough for today.

Do the same thing tomorrow and the next day, making a total of eighteen times that you have talked through that speech, and Mister, you have earned permission from the Noble Knights of Power Speaking to charge an honorarium for your work at the podium. You will have a polished speech.

Now get up there and do a great job on the platform and, no matter how skinny your shoulders or how wobbly your legs, the doors won't be wide enough to accommodate the exodus that will go bolting forth to answer your challenge when you pop your proposal.

Some of the world's most powerful speakers were little guys determined to equalize their small stature with a great big mouth.

POURING WORDS OUT IN A STEADY STREAM

The words that pour from your oral cavity during your performance as you describe the string of pictures traveling across your mental screen will be almost the same words you used when you talked out your speech to yourself, because you have only so many words in your speaking vocabulary. But you did not memorize *words*—except those on your outline —*you memorized pictures*.

The words you use on the platform are actually the words you use in daily conversation. In chatting with your fellow man you don't think with words, you think with pictures and the words flow naturally. As you deliver a speech your oral pictures, which you have already arranged beforehand, come tumbling along in orderly fashion and the words to describe them flow easily—provided you are not *word-conscious* as you speak.

Delivering a speech can be not only the easiest job a man will ever do but also the most rewarding, because it will heap upon his skinny shoulders and wobbly legs the respect of his boss and his fellow workers and his customers and his wife and his kids and anyone else he would like to impress. It will get him a nice raise in salary plus maybe a trip to Hawaii for the whole "famn damily."

HOW TO MAKE YOUR WORDS SINCERE

Every audience wants to hear the words that flowed naturally into the speaker's mind while he was preparing his speech, because these are *feeling* words, *sincere* words, words that are a real part of the speaker himself—not a piece of the dictionary hurled at them. These words *are* the speaker. If you happen to hire some rawboned rascal from the boondocks to come and address your university club on "The Preservation of the Prowling Panther" and he comes bowlegging to the microphone and tries to sound like a college professor just because you are paying him a big honorarium, the noise that issues from that man's mouth is artificial, the palooka is a fake and a flop: "Back to the boondocks, Rawboned Rascal!"

We have almost a million words in the English language. You probably carry about 75,000 of them in your reading vocabulary, 35,000 in your listening vocabulary, 15,000 in your writing vocabulary, but only about 8,000 in your speaking vocabulary. Why not add another thousand or so to your speaking repertory? It's really not *that* hard to do—not if you go for little words that snap and crackle and pop. Cut a big word in two and you get two little words. Cut a little word and it bleeds, because little words have a heart beat. Big words lost their lives back when Julius Caesar was hammering his exciting way up and down the roadways of the known world and later writing out his reports in Latin that put people to sleep.

The King James version of the Bible uses about 6,000 different words. That's all! The Bible was spoken before it was written. It is a speaker's Bible. Thousands of vivid pictures pass before the mind's eye as you read it. The Twenty-Third Psalm is one vivid picture tumbling after another right down to the very end. The average word in the Bible is only two syllables long. Yet the Holy Scriptures rank among the best in world literature. Billy Graham has the finest text book on Power Speaking known to man.

LITTLE WORDS THAT BLEED WHEN CUT

Whether you are a butcher or a baker or a college professor—or a rawbone rascal from the boondocks—you don't have to talk like this:

"I received your most interesting communication in today's postal delivery."

Why don't you just come straight out with it:

"Hey, man, I just got your letter and it's a pee dinger!"

Slang is absolutely okay if it communicates the clear, vivid picture. Slang used often enough becomes idiomatic expression. Idioms used often enough worm their ornery way into the King's English.

Let's go for the verb. Let's suppress the adjective and the adverb. The really great parts of speech are the noun and the verb. These two are the bones of verbal expression, the skeleton that holds the body of our language together. The noun tells who did it and the verb shows what he did.

Rattle those bones. If you are telling about some immigrating pilgrim who goes perambulating down the street, let him *stagger*, *stumble*, or *strut;* or *wobble*, *wiggle* or *scoot;* and when he arrives at his destination let him *flounder*, *flip*, or *flop;* but, for Heaven's sake, don't keep him forevermore peregrinating down the street. *Rattle those bones.* Any time some big, fat verb of over two syllables comes crawling into your mind, make the thing pay to get in, and then let it in only when you cannot find a smaller gem that will show a better picture.

Little words are like David, small and agile and scantily clad—easy to see. Big words are like Goliath, huge and clumsy and hidden in armor—hard to fathom.

So, Mr. Power Speaker now comes the time to crank up your courage because we are approaching the podium where we will shortly square off against a big audience. I will be happy to introduce you if you will make the speech.

18

POWER SPEAKING THE WAY
LISTENERS LIKE IT

"Ladies and gentlemen, I take great pleasure in presenting to you now for your listening pleasure, Mr. Power Speaker."

Are you nervous, Mr. Speaker? You had better be. A race horse is nervous as he nears the starting gate. An All-American halfback is nervous as the kick-off nears his throbbing fingers. Of course a cow is not the least bit nervous as the milkmaid nears the barn. But the race horse and the halfback will put on a great show while the cow will be a miserable flop at the box office.

You had better be nervous. Nervousness means your feeling-brain is jumping with excitement and squirting your internal workings with adrenalin which, until you get into action, will make your knees quiver and your fingers throb and your stomach flutter. But once in action you will feel your entire system humming with the thrilling experience.

"Were you nervous before your speech?" you ask a friend
of yours who has just done a great job on the platform.

"No, not the least bit," beams the lying devil.

"Then how come I saw you sneaking out of the ladies'
rest-room just before they called on you!"

MAKING THEM LOOK AND LISTEN

If you are nervous you are ready to speak. But is the audience
ready? Maybe yes, maybe no. Your first job is to make sure
those people out there start listening when you start talking.
All people everywhere come to play, so the moment you arrive
at the podium start putting the audience on your team. Don't
say anything for a moment. Just look around from side to side
and front to back. Gaze into their eyes. Smile. If your adrenalin
is squirting, your smile will sparkle. There is no such thing
as a homely smile. You will look good. Now let's hear you
sound good:

"Thank you, Mr. Toastmaster, good evening, ladies and
gentlemen . . ."

Go immediately into your speech. Do not roam with your
sparkling orbs up and down the head table saluting all the important people sitting there. It's not your job to introduce the dig-
nitaries. Somebody else will do that. If you start saluting the
head table, the audience will look along with you and they may
find somebody there more interesting than you. They just may
forget to come back to you. Goliath may have your head with
the first swipe of his thirty-pound sword. Keep those people
looking at you. You are the main attraction for the next half-hour.

Let yourself go. Say things the way you feel them. The
nervousness you felt when the toastmaster was calling you to
the microphone has now turned into enthusiasm and pep and
punch. Let your gestures come and go as they will. Don't hold

them back. Don't push them forward. Just let them flow the way they want to go. They will flow the way you feel. You will find yourself pounding your palm to hammer a strong point home. You will stick three fingers toward the ceiling when you want to count off three categories. You will straight-arm your audience with the heel of your hand when you want to warn them against some lurking Goliath. These gestures simply come naturally when you feel what you are saying.

"I want a speaker to look like a man fighting a swarm of bees," said one of America's original Power Speakers—Abraham Lincoln by name.

SPEAKING THAT'S EASY AND FUN TO DO

When you deliver your body along with your speech, the great thunderbolt of persuasive speaking known as the Power of Suggestion will send an electrifying current throughout the audience and set them throbbing upright in their chairs.

Millions of people the country over subscribe to the many public speaking courses offered throughout the nation every year, and all come away from those courses better speakers. But only a few thousand become great speakers. And only a few hundred become Power Speakers. Yet Power Speaking is easy to learn and fun to do for three reasons:

1. You see what you say.
2. You feel what you speak.
3. And you let your whole body do your talking.

FIGHTING AN UGLY THING CALLED FEAR

Here is the greatest mystery of modern times: Why are there not more Power Speakers? A big, rawboned country preacher up in Calhoun County taught me the answer years ago:

"Too many speakers are *afraid to let themselves go* on the platform."

They hold themselves back. They don't permit themselves to feel what they are saying. They put the brakes on their emotions.

'Tis an ugly thing called fear. Before them sits a wide-eyed audience that yearns to be motivated, human beings eager for a better, more thrilling way to spend these few short years here on this mortal coil. The speaker may have a fine speech but if he fails to deliver it with his entire body, his message will fail to get across—all because he is *afraid*. His feeling-brain whimpers like a beaten dog and sneaks off into the darkest recesses of his cranium. As surely as the Great Jehovah sits upon his Heavenly throne, there's only one way to lick fear and that is to *go into action*. Don't just stand there—do something. *Let yourself go!*

DAMMIT TO HELL WHERE'S MY POWER

Nervousness is a wonderful asset. It fills your entire body with an electric current that sends your message zooming down from the podium or across the dinner table or over the boss's desk. Nervousness turns you into an exciting fellow who is fun to be around.

Fear destroys you. It shuts off your juices. It takes the sparkle from your eyes. It hangs your arms down limp at your side.

"Somebody please call me a funeral," you seem to be saying as you stand there apparently hopeless and helpless. There is hope, mister, and there is help.

Dale Carnegie probably developed more Power Speakers in his speech courses than did any other mortal man. One of the biggest problems he encountered was a brilliant young scientist who had a way of standing before the class like a concrete telephone pole and delivering his speech in a dreary monotone.

"Put some feeling into what you're saying," said Carnegie.

The scientist droned wearily on.

"Let yourself go," pleaded Dale.

The speaker blinked once but that was the only change.

"Sock it to 'em!" roared the persistent instructor.

"Dammit to hell, *I can't do it!*" shrieked the frustrated scientist as he smashed his fist into his palm, sent a vicious kick at the speaker's stand, and strode angrily from the platform with these words:

"You can take your speech course and shove it down your alimentary canal!"

"No," smiled Dale Carnegie, the great teacher of Power Speaking, "I think we'll keep right on with the course because *we have just developed a brand new Power Speaker!* Congratulations!"

Dale Carnegie was a little guy who could hardly knock you down with his small bony fist, but he knew how to banish your stage fright and make you turn on Power and speak with your entire body.

MAKING YOUR FEARS GO DOWN THE DRAIN

You can cure your nervousness by stepping to the microphone and turning that nervousness into enthusiasm. You can cure your fear by *acting* confidently. Your feeling-brain is easy to fool. The stronger your fear and *the more confidently you act*, the greater the burst of nervous energy and the stronger the surge of speaking Power that will gush from your gullible feeling-brain.

Susie McGoosie, the Belle of the Calhoun County Fair, fell into the bull pen, and she ran, screaming for her life. She did not run because she was *afraid*. She ran because she was *nervous*. She was not afraid until she was safe and sound. Then she fainted, because her feeling-brain shrank away and turned off her juices the moment she started to feel fear.

TALKING THEM OUT OF THEIR PANTS

You are not afraid as you approach the microphone. You are nervous. You are not afraid until you look out into that great sea of faces and find yourself eyeball to eyeball with the monster called Goliath who sits out there waving his thirty-pound sword. But you don't have to be afraid even then, not if you will put on a show of confidence and let yourself go and speak with your entire body.

Suppose you are to speak before the boss and all the other top brass in the organization. How does a fellow crank up a show of confidence in full view of all those important people? Simple. Just say to yourself something like the following as you wait to be introduced:

1. These guys put their pants on the same way I do, one leg at a time.
2. Each of these birds owes me a thousand bucks. (Fool your feeling-brain.)
3. Look at the poor devils—they forgot to wear their pants today!
4. I'm going to deliver this speech the way I see it and the way I feel it if it's the last thing I ever do on this earth.
5. Go get 'em, Tiger!

19

POWER SPEAKING'S FINEST FRIEND

When you were a child you spoke as a child but your tones were clear as a silver bell. You could yell all day and bawl half the night and bounce out of bed the next morning with a voice stronger than ever. The muscles of your throat, like those elsewhere in your tiny body, were soft and pliable, permitting the three megaphones of your voice box, which are the cavities of the nose, the mouth, and the throat, to function wide open so that your syllables came out round and smooth and mellow. Your voice was a music box.

Then you became a man and you put away childish things. Did you put away the music box? Some people do. The tones that in childhood were so pleasant to a listener's ear may have now grown nasal or screeching or gutteral or any two or all three. Can you deliver a Power Speech today and tomorrow and the next day without being hoarse for a week? Can you

yell out the kitchen window at your kids over on the next street
without your voice slipping down the drain? If you cannot, then
you need to go looking for your childhood music box. It is
still there right where you left it, but you may have to uncover
it.

What actually happened was that a voice-pirate by the name
of Goliath came lurking out of the darkness and inflicted upon
you a bad habit called *pinched throat*. Power Speaking's greatest
enemy is *pinched throat*. You may come to the podium with
the finest speech in all the land, but if you deliver it with *pinched
throat* you won't sound good, and three days in a row at the
microphone will lay you up for a week with laryngitis. Your
voice will slide down the drain.

SOUNDING YOUR SYLLABLES THE POWER WAY

There is one sure cure for *pinched throat* and only one.
It is called *open throat*. The throat is the doorway through which
the voice must pass. The more open the door, the m re voice
that passes through. An *open throat* permits your *ing* and your
ong and your *ung* sounds to go up high in the nasal cavity and
come out pure and beautiful, but a *pinched throat* makes you
sound like a speaker with a cold in the head. An *open throat*
rolls your long *o* around in your mouth and sends it out in a
perfect circle, while a *pinched throat* squeezes it through in a
squashed-down oval. An *open throat* sounds your long *i* like
eye, while a *pinched throat* makes it come out like the second
a in jack*a*ss. But best of all an *open throat* enables you to speak
on and on until doomsday without showing the least sign of laryngitis.

MAKING THE MOST OF THE VOICE YOU HAVE

The voice you have is good enough for Power Speaking. History is full of cases featuring public speakers who were bothered with *pinched throat*. Demosthenes filled his mouth full of stones and shouted from the shores of the Aegean Sea until his throat came open and stayed open while he talked. Lincoln's voice at first was a nasal tenor but he worked on it until it was described later as a "clear trumpet that can be heard from a great distance." Half the people who mount speaker's platforms have better voices than Charles Laughton, but few make their words pay off better than did this great actor. The finest Power Speaker of the Twentieth Century, Winston Churchill, had trouble enunciating his *s*'s, but his voice packed power because he spoke with an *open throat*.

HOW TO DEVELOP AN OPEN THROAT

When O. J. Simpson took the pitchout from his quarterback in the Rose Bowl and left our fine Ohio State team stretched out on the ground behind him while he raced on for eighty yards and a touchdown, he glided past our bench with his *mouth hanging open and his jaw flopping loose*. Running in front of a hundred thousand people who stomped the stands with their feet and split the sky with their voices, while a hundred million more sat electrified all about the nation with their eyes glued on their television sets, "Orange Juice" Simpson *performed with an open throat*. A professional player now, O. J. spends his time in the off-season making television movies. He speaks with a beautiful baritone voice. No wonder: *he performs with an open throat*.

How do you speak with an *open throat?* There's just one way: *relax your jaw and let it hang loose on its hinges, and talk.* Whether you are speaking to one person or a hundred or a thousand, *relax your jaw and let it hang loose on its hinges, and talk.* Why did I repeat that statement? Because it spells out the cure. Because Power Speaking's greatest enemy is *pinched throat.* Because Power Speaking's greatest friend is *open throat.* Therefore if you want to address your son down in the next block, you had better relax your jaw and let it hang loose on its hinges and *yell.* If you tighten your throat muscles thinking to make a louder sound, your voice will not carry so far nor will your voice-box feel so good afterward. The secret of voice projection is simply to send more air through the vocal cords but *perform with an open throat.* Then you can yell until Judgment Day and still have enough voice left to plead your case before the Judge.

Power Speaking's Greatest Enemy

I stood one evening at a podium in Cleveland, Ohio, before one thousand Turf Builders of America and tore into them with Woody's old fighting phrase, "Sock it to 'em, knock 'em down, hit!" and, brother, my voice went down the drain. Goliath had my head in his pocket. For the first time in thirty-eight years of podium pounding I lost my voice. I drank half a glass of cold water and finished my speech with one fourth of a voice. I was much chagrined. When the treasurer handed me the check for the honorarium I hesitated—but I took it.

I will never let that scene be repeated, though. I learned a lesson right then and right there that I have known for years: *relax the jaw and let it hang loose on its hinges and yell.* Every athletic coach knows that a relaxed muscle will stretch like a rubber band but a tense muscle won't stretch at all—it will tear. I knew that. I also know this: The vocal cords are not cords, they are muscles, and if you keep them loose they will stretch and vibrate and hum a pretty tune, but if you tense them up they will strain and rip and tear and your voice will slide down the drain.

A VICIOUS HABIT EASILY CURED

When you stand up and speak, most of your nervousness that shows on the outside will disappear if you will simply *relax your jaw and let it hang loose on its hinges*. If you are full of fright, you will not be able to relax your jaw until you put on a show of confidence and dispel your fears.

Some people even in conversation suffer from *pinched throat* every time they open their mouths. This bad habit can become vicious, but it can be broken much more easily than many other bad habits. All in the world a person needs to do is to put his thinking-brain in charge of his daily conversation at home, in the office, on the street, for a little while, and make that thinking-brain keep issuing the following orders: Relax the jaw and let it hang loose on its hinges—then talk.

20

WINNING YOUR WAY WITHOUT HOGGING THE BALL

Suppose you are the representative from the labor gang called in to sit among a roomful of company big-shots holding a conference on overtime in the steel mill. Today you will get a chance to make a second kind of Power Speech. There are three kinds: the Platform Speech which you have already mastered, the Conference Comment which you will make today, and the Speech of Introduction which we will discuss in the following chapter. After that, you will be able to live out your life packing a secret weapon known as Power Speaking.

Today is a new experience: the Conference Comment. You don't have weeks to work this one out the way you did with your Platform Speech. You have to start thinking right now.

RUBBING ELBOWS WITH THE GREAT

"Should I just sit here and listen and learn and not take part?"

Not on your life, Man! Not if you expect to rise in this business. Not if you expect to rise in any business. Here is a great opportunity. You are rubbing elbows today with the leaders of this organization. But don't forget they put their pants on one leg at a time just like you. Their total brains weigh three pounds apiece just like yours. Their thinking-brains weigh only five ounces—just like yours. This is a meeting of the minds. Everybody here has one responsibility: *to take part*. From the combined thinking of this whole group must come a vital decision about requiring the men to work overtime.

BLOWING YOUR CHANCE WITH TOO EARLY A BLAST

What is the first thing you would do, Mr. Labor Representative? Would you jump to your feet early in the meeting and start talking?

"Keep compulsory overtime the hell out of the steel mill because . . ."

Wow! You smacked them right between the eyes with your proposal the very moment you parted your pulsating lips, didn't you? The boss said he called this meeting to *discuss* and *decide*—discuss *first* and *then* decide. You sound like your decision is made and to heck with what anybody else thinks and "Let's get the thunder back to work!" Your eagerness to get back to work may impress the boss, but you may never leave that particular job. Do you know what the wise old heads around the room are thinking?

"Back to the boondocks, Rawhide Rascal!"

No, in a Conference Comment you save your proposal until the last. The first thing you do is establish your theme in your own mind as quickly as you can. Work it out so that you can say it in *one unforgettable sentence.* Make it *easy* to understand and *congenial* to hear—for everybody there regardless of how he happens to stand on the issue at stake.

SOUNDING THREE THEMES WITH ONE BREATH

Here is another big no-no:

"Mr. Chairman, in the first place the furnace room of a steel mill is too dangerous, in the second place the work is too hard, and in the third place   . ."

Hold it! You are hogging the ball, Slugger! You are sounding *three* themes. You are cranking up to speak all afternoon. These are important men! Their time is valuable. Everybody here wants a chance to speak. This is not one speaker and an audience. These people are all speakers. What will they think of you?

"Back to the labor yard, Ball-hogging Buster!"

No, you start off by sounding *one definite theme at a time.* If you want to make another point wait until your turn comes again and then make another speech. If you want to make a third point make a third speech—when your turn comes. *In a conference use the Single-Shot, never the Scatter-Gun.*

COMING BACK STRONG WITH A WAY-OUT THEME

Suppose you work out something like this:

"Mr. Chairman, I quote from Alfred Lord Bodiddle Brown: A furnace room is one hell of a place to get sleepy."

Boy, oh, boy! What a frivolous phrase! Right! But you just wager your bottom peso that a *frivolous phrase can drive home serious thoughts.* So out with it. Speak it!

Whereas in a platform speech you would now put the theme into action with a word picture to explain it, in a Conference Comment you leap immediately into the development, using the Single-Shot method.

Go on talking:

"I have gathered statistics covering the past ten years. For every hundred million dollars worth of steel poured in the steel mill we have lost a man's life. For every ten million dollars worth somebody has lost an arm or a leg. And for every million dollars somebody has given up a finger or a toe.

"Certainly the steel mill pays the highest wages in the country and certainly some of the guys love those fat paychecks, but, gentlemen, let's be realistic: the steel mill is too dangerous for long hours.

"Therefore, I urge you to cast a stone at this Goliath who stands before us by voting to keep compulsory overtime out of the steel mill."

Your way-out theme has been phrased in light-hearted words, but those words have concealed a serious point that came charging home to your listeners as you dramatize your statistics, so that when you popped your proposal your little speech made a lot of good, common sense. Phrasing your theme in light-hearted words spoken sincerely to convey a serious thought builds up a contrast, and contrasts pack a wallop.

OUTLINE FOR A CONFERENCE COMMENT

A Conference Comment proceeds according to the following outline:

1. Sound your theme.
2. Develop your theme with one good illustration.
3. Echo your theme.
4. Pop your proposal.
5. Sit down.

Another way of taking part in a conference discussion is to listen carefully to the comments made by other members. Somebody on the same side of the question as you is sure to sound a theme that will attract a vivid illustration from your memory storehouse.

You can then get the floor following this co-fellow's speech and announce your theme as follows:

"Mr. Chairman, I would like to support the point just made by Mr. Rockefelloford, because . . ."

You not only have made a new friend in Mr. Rockefelloford but you have also added fuel to your own fire-power.

Caution! If you take exception to some speaker on the opposite side of the question and come roaring to your feet with a rousing rebuttal of his speech that packs so much punch that you threaten to throw this conference into a bull session of "cussing and discussing," the loud rap! rap! rap! of the boss's gavel means:

"Back to the sweat shop, Obstreperous Lapel Grabber!"

Persuasion—not dissuasion—remember? Any time you feel compelled to refute some statement made by a fellow conferee, the very first thing you should do is to let that conferee know what a fine fellow you think he is and then what a lousy idea he has come up with. Attack the idea, not the man. As Dale Carnegie would say it, "Lather the man before you shave him." As Tiger Ellison puts it: Don't stick your finger under a man's nose and glare at him eyeball to eyeball and tell him what a miserable mess he is for taking such an attitude, but rather stand beside him man to man, shoulder to shoulder, and point out to him what a miserable mess his idea would lead to. Put your heart in your voice. Let him see your soul in your eyes. You may not make a friend this way but at least you will not lose his respect. If you don't feel opposed that strongly to his idea, forget it. If you can't score a point or two for your side, let it go. Get on with your positive punching. Sell your own themes and let his lie unsold on the podium because yours are better, not because his are worse. His respect for you will grow greater, and you possibly could have made a friend. Persuasion—not dissuasion—because *persuasion is Power*.

GOOD LIFE THAT GETS BETTER

Anytime you look good and sound good making a Conference Comment, regardless of whether the ballot later favors your proposal or opposes it, the other members of that conference will be impressed by your show of leadership, and you will be called on for future assignments that will make life a little better and a bit more thrilling for you and yours.

Good luck with your Conference Comments.

21

HELPING THE SPEAKER
START OFF RIGHT

"Hey, Joe, we want you to come to the banquet just to enjoy yourself this time. We're not asking you to make another speech. But we would like you to introduce the speaker!"

Don't ever let anybody tell you that introducing the speaker is not making a speech. It takes a good speech, a Power Speech, one that you have to work on, but one that will not only benefit the person you are introducing—it will also boost old Number One himself.

Your speech of introduction should be short but it ought to be good. Your purpose as an intruducer is to help the speaker get off to a flying start. When you finish introducing him you should hand him over to a big-eyed audience who, though they appreciate you, will now be eager to listen to this main attraction.

OH HOW DIRTY CAN YOU GET

You can play a dirty trick on the main speaker by stealing the show. You can take ten minutes and give these people a little verbal humdinger of your own which will thrill them so much that they will now turn their attention to the main speaker with a look that challenges him to do as well.

"Let's see you top that, Rawbone Rascal!" they seem to be thinking as the poor speaker pauses at the podium and looks his audience over.

If you do steal the show, Mr. Power Introducer, you had better prepare your coat lapels for some serious hand-grabbing because even though you sneak away and build your home in the depths of the woods, the Noble Knights of Power Speaking will send their tail-twister beating a path to your door.

You can also play a dirty trick on the speaker by introducing him with all the pompous power you possess so that the poor guy just absolutely cannot come up to the picture you paint of him. His speech may not be too bad. In fact it may be pretty good except for one thing—the contrast between the picture you painted and the picture they got packed such a wallop that the audience went home disappointed. Again the tail-twister cometh.

SETTING HIM UP AND KNOCKING HIM DOWN

You are pulling a third dirty trick when at the end of your Speech of Introduction, as the speaker comes to attention with both hands against the edge of the table ready to push off and spring to the microphone, you pull the trigger of your starting pistol and then call him back to his mark:

"So I take great pleasure in presenting Mr. Bodiddly Brown (Bodiddly springs to his feet) . . . a man who has proved by the way he has lived his life (Bodiddly sinks sadly back into his chair) . . . that he is capable of being Governor of this great state—Mr. Bodiddly Brown." (Bodiddly comes cautiously to his feet.)

In a Speech of Introduction don't even mention the speaker's name until your very last words in your very last statement. When you arrive at that last sentence look straight into the faces of the audience and speak it like this:

"Ladies and Gentlemen, I present to you (slight pause) MR. BODDIDDLY BROWN!"

Speak his name slowly, distinctly, forcefully. Then turn and look at Mr. Brown and stretch one arm toward him, palm upward, and wait for him to take over the microphone before you leave. Leaving the podium before the speaker gets there is desertion. It fills the room with dead air. It gives the audience a chance to sneak a peek at the full-bosomed waitresses. How is Bodiddly ever going to get these healthy male animals to look at him again? Also—you never know—something could happen to Bodiddly on his way up and you may have to spend the rest of the evening at the microphone yourself. So, Mr. Power Introducer, stand guard at the podium until the speaker arrives.

THIS ONE THING AND NOTHING MORE

Any time you make a Speech of Introduction you have only one proposal in mind: to focus the eyes and ears of the audience on the speaker from the start. That and nothing more. All he can ask of you and all you should ever attempt to do is give him a wide-awake audience looking at him and ready to listen.

"Here then, Mr. Main Speaker," you are saying to yourself as you stretch forth an arm beckoning him to come, "is your audience. I have prepared them for the kill. From now on it's Little You against Big Them. Hit 'em in the eye and stick 'em in the heart. Good luck."

Here's the outline for a Speech of Introduction:

1. Sound your theme: "Our speaker is a strong man with a courageous heart and a fine feeling for folks."
2. Develop your theme: Tell them how Bodiddly armed only with a three-legged camp stool rushed into a cave full of wildcats and rescued Mrs. Shagnasty's youngster, Baby Boy Broderick.
3. Echo your theme.
4. Hand the speaker over to the audience.

LOOKING GOOD AND SOUNDING GREAT

The Noble Knights are proud to have you as one of their members. They will always be pulling for you to look good and sound great whether you are giving a Platform Speech, a Conference Comment, or a Speech of Introduction. You never make them shudder with such beat up expressions as "It is indeed a pleasure" (Oh, how trite! trite! trite!) . . . "a man who needs no introduction" (The hell he doesn't! Everybody does! Even the President!) . . . "I would be remiss if" (Worn out! Used up! All gone!) . . . "I am reminded of a story" (You had it in mind all along, you rawboned rascal!) . . . "it seems that there were three old maids" (It seems, but dammit are you sure!) . . . and so on *ad nauseum.*

When you make a speech you use the nice little words that come sparkling up out of your memory storehouse as you look at the mental pictures you have planned for your audience.

If you use clichés—and I hope you do—I'm willing to wager my next honorarium that you use the ones that still have snap, crackle, and pop:

> "Hot in the heart . . . boiling in the blood . . . lower the boom . . . a real hornet's nest . . . fell flat on his foolish face . . . a tight jam . . . maybe it will blow over . . . ran like a scared rabbit . . . scampered like a scalded cat . . . took off like a big-butted baboon . . . fit as a fiddle . . . brown as a berry . . . hard as a rock . . . hotter than the hinges of Hades . . . cool, calm, and collected . . . proud as a peacock . . . blown in by the four winds of Heaven . . . North, South, East, West, sideways and crooked . . . root, hog, or die . . . dig little pig, or starve to death . . . dainty as a dew lily . . . knee-bent and body-bowed . . . hogwash and pig slop . . . built like a brick outhouse . . . tall hog at the trough . . . Well, I'm a suck-egg mule!"

Good clichés are picturesque tidbits that communicate right now because they originally came popping from the hearts of people who were feeling something way down deep while the words were being uttered. Never shy away from any expression that communicates. That is what the language is all about.

WHY THEY WANT YOU ON THE PROGRAM

Another reason those people wanted you on the program, even though they already had a main speaker, was that you never apologize:

> "Pardon me for being late but . . ." (Sounds so weak!)
> "Please excuse my husky voice but . . ." (Brace up, fellow!)
> "I'm sorry I didn't have time to prepare a speech . . ." (How embarrassing!)

If you were to apologize for being late or for having a cold or for not being prepared, the audience would shift about in their uncomfortable seats and make wry faces. They would look at you as if you were standing up there wearing smoked glasses and holding out a tin cup for alms. Some of them might toss you a nickle and then start making eyes at the full-bosomed waitresses. Do you realize what you would be doing to your feeling-brain? The great watchdog of persuasion known as the Power of Suggestion would send your feeling-brain running for cover. Your juices would slow down. Your energy would ooze to a trickle. Your picture-popping apparatus would grow sluggish. You would not look good standing up there, nor would you sound good. Thank goodness, you do not apologize to audiences, whether you are introducing the main speaker or whether you are the big attraction yourself.

Regardless of conditions you are a positive puncher. Congratulations!

22

CONVERSING WITH POWER AMONG YOUR FELLOWS

> "The time has come," the Walrus said,
> "To talk of many things:
> Of shoes—and ships—and sealing wax—
> Of cabbages—and kings—"*

Up in Calhoun County lived a fellow by the name of Horatio Jones who was forever embarrassed about two things: first, his right leg, which was six inches shorter than his left, and second, his only son, who stuttered.

> "Sa-hah-sa-hay-say, Dad," said the boy eagerly one day.
> "Yes, son?" said Horatio.
> "I know a wa-hah-wa-hay-way you can wa-hah-

---

* L. Carroll, *Alice Through the Looking-Glass*.

wa-haw-walk down town wi-tha-wi-thou-without getting embarrassed.''

"How's that, boy?''

"Wa-hah-wa-haw-walk with your left leg in the gu-hah-gu-huh-gutter and your right leg on the cu-hah-cu-huh-curb.''

The old man nodded and decided to try the youngster's plan. However the scheme backfired when Horatio, walking smoothly along the curb with half his torso protruding in the street, suddenly was side-swiped by a hot-rodding teenager in a souped-up jalopy.

The son came to the hospital to visit his father.

"I'm shu-huh-shu-hoo-sure sorry about that bro-huh-bro-hoh-broken leg, Dad.''

"Oh, that's all right, boy,'' said Horatio. "You youngsters are only trying to help us old folks. And now I want to help you. I know how to stop your stuttering.''

"Oh, good, Dad! How?''

"Just keep your *damn mouth shut!*''

All of which is a doubtful way to stop stuttering but a sure-fire way to stop conversation, and our country surely does need more and better conversation.

What to Say Among Strangers

"I don't know what to say among strangers,'' says Elmer Shy Guy.

If Elmer lived here on our little island just off the coast he could talk about the weather because we are the storm capital of the world. Elmer could tell you about water spouts that come whirling in off the Gulf of Mexico spinning a column of water six hundred feet high and carving a saucer in the surface of the Old Devil Sea fifty feet across and twenty-five feet deep.

He could talk to you about cranking speckled trout and flounder and sand perch into our back yard from out of the Gulf that would make a fisherman's eyes bug out like billiard balls.

He could tell you about roaming the sugar-white sand beaches of this island and picking up a thousand varieties of sea shells. He could talk to you about swimming too far off shore and suddenly spying the ominous fin of a tiger shark cruising in from the sea.

He could talk about losing eight golf balls in Boca Ciega Bay while shooting eighteen holes on our local course. He could talk about bucking the waves in the Gulf of Mexico in a twenty-foot outboard. Elmer would have plenty to talk about here. But Elmer has plenty to talk about *wherever he is!* And so have you, Mr. Power Conversationalist!

Stuff That Anybody Will Listen to

"But people aren't interested in what I have to say," moans Elmer.

Nonsense. People are interested in anything that thrills them, and listening to anybody speak on any subject that he feels deeply about, relating the way he feels, becomes a thrilling experience, because the great watchdog of persuasive speaking, known as the Power of Suggestion, makes the listener's juices flow. He can't escape. He identifies with the enthusiastic talker. He becomes the speaker in his heart. His adrenalin squirts and his energy burns and pictures pop from out of his past so that he can hardly wait to take over the role of speaker when his turn comes. People become so interested in anything spoken with feeling that they want to return the compliment with feeling. This is conversation.

Knocking the Shyness Out of Elmer

"But I'm too shy," says Elmer.

Now you're talking, Mr. Elmer Shy Guy. You should spell your middle name with *sh* and then add *i*. The *sh* stands for *shush* and the *i* means *you*, Elmer. Do you know what makes you so shy? You won't stop thinking about *you!* There's only one way on God's green earth to stop being shy and that's to stop thinking about yourself and start thinking about *somebody else* or *some other thing*.

Elmer, I know a good way to make you stop thinking about yourself. If I haul off and sock you in the kisser with my bony fist, you'll start thinking about *me*. I'll be at the top of your list of things to think about. But I don't want to fight you, Elmer. I just want to hear you talk.

If I stand beside you man to man, shoulder to shoulder, and point out to you what a miserable mess you make standing there sucking your thumb while other fellows at the party are spewing and spouting exciting conversation, maybe you will recoil from the miserable mess you are making and bounce toward what you ought to be doing: Making conversation.

What should Elmer talk about? He could talk about what he saw and heard on television the other night. All Elmer has to do is step up to his set, twist a little knob, and lay the whole world out before his eyes and ears. Television need not be a boob tube, for it can bring into your living room and mine—and Elmer's—some of the most exciting stuff happening in the world today. Whether what you see and hear makes you mad or glad or sad or tingle with whatever emotion you like to tingle with, it brings you something to converse about among your fellows.

If you and I had a penny for every newspaper and magazine and paperback book and hardback that flood the market today, we could buy out the Rockefellers and the Vanderbilts and have enough left over for a couple of plane tickets around the world first class—and we could even stick Elmer in the front row alongside of us. Modern man has more to talk about than any other mortal since the beginning of time.

DRAWING YOUR LISTENER INTO YOUR TALK

Some conversations are better than others. If you listen to a tape recording of the talk that takes place among you and a carload of the boys from the office as you drive down one of our superhighways heading for the Annual Company Conference several hours away, you will be amazed. How often the subject changes! How often somebody butts in on somebody else! How often the fellows in the back seat talk about something at the same time those in the front seat talk about something else! What a mess! Unless you have on board *a Power Conversationalist who is willing to take charge.*

There's one big difference between public speaking and conversation: In conversation the speaker trades places with the listener over and over again and again. A Power Conversationalist operates exactly the way he does in a Conference Comment—he states a theme and then he develops it with a word picture. Having made his point he awaits further development by his fellows. He gives them a chance to become speakers. Even though he may be the most exciting man in the group he does not hog the show. If he fails to get a reaction from his mates on the point he wants discussed, he may put the spurs to them thus:

"What would you fellows think if . . . ?" or "In your
opinion what . . . ?" or "Do you guys know of other cases
where . . . ?"

HERE IS POWER CONVERSATION

In a conversation, a good speaker will cause your feeling-
brain to pop pictures upon your mental screen that you are eager
to talk about. You can go barging in while the speaker's mouth
is wide-open and jump right down his throat with your comments.
It's being done everywhere. It's one of the best ways known
to man to make yourself unwanted in any group. Or you can
stand there bug-eyed and eager, watching and waiting, drinking
in every word the speaker utters, soaking up every phrase, until
you get a chance to talk. If you do await your turn, your eagerness
will draw out the best that is in the speaker, and if he is as
good as he sounds, he will stop after one illustration of his point
and give you a turn at bat. He will hold back other vivid word-
pictures until his turn comes again. This is conversation the way
the good Lord intended it to be—passing the word back and
forth with everybody playing the game. This is Power Conversation.

WORD-BOMBERS WHO SPEAK WITH FOG-HORN VOICES

If you are interested in a point being made by another member
of your group and some obstreperous word-bomber comes thun-
dering in with his fog-horn voice and captures the center of
the stage with an entirely new thought, you have a perfect right
to speak up in the manner of a man taking charge:

"Wait just a dad-burn minute! I want to hear what Bodiddly
was talking about . . . !"

Even the rascal who butted in on Bodiddly will have to respect you for taking charge because nothing is more ridiculous than conversation constantly interrupted.

If some argument-loving cuss shows up in your group and takes the opposite view on everything said just for the pure hell of it, you'll know next time whom not to invite when you drive a carload to the Annual Company Convention. One argument lover can take all the fun out of a trip—two can wreck the car.

STEERING CLEAR OF THINGS TABOO

There are three subjects that are absolutely taboo during an automobile trip to the Annual Company Convention: politics, race, and religion, unless all of you are either Republican or Democrat or Activist and belong to the same race and the same church. A difference here becomes a squabble which leads to a quarrel which ends in a fight. Politics or race or religion can bring civilized man down upon all fours, growling like a berserk bull. Mr. Power Conversationalist, let's see you take charge:

"Gentlemen, there are three subjects that are absolutely taboo in this automobile and they are *politics, race,* and *religion.*"

PUTTING SOME WARMTH INTO YOUR WORDS

Oscar Hammerstein sat watching the audience during the early days of the musical, *The King and I,* which he and Richard Rodgers had adapted from the book, *Anna and the King of Siam.* Oscar sat with his chin cupped in one hand and his eyes glued on the faces of the paying customers. The audience seemed interested enough but they sat stone-faced. The play needed something. It was too cold. Suddenly he had it! What is the one thing that will warm up any audience?

Hammerstein and Rodgers proceeded to write into *The King and I* the scene where the King holds out his hand to Anna and asks her to show him the steps of the polka. Then as the two sing "Shall We Dance" he sweeps her into the dance with his arm about her waist. Not a torrid love scene, no, but a little romance that warmed the audience and headed *The King and I* toward greatness.

Anything you can offer with feeling in a conversation will, through the Power of Suggestion, tend to make your listeners feel the same way. Anything that thrills you and makes you tingle belongs in the category of romance, the third greatest cause for action that burns in the human breast. You really don't need Anna or the King or even the King's full-bosomed daughter to warm yourself romantically. Any thrilling experience sparkles with romance. It could be a ten-pound bass on the end of your fly rod. It could be a small motorboat riding for shore two thirds of the way up the back of a twenty-foot wave. Or it could be the King's daughter. Relate a thrilling experience with the same warm emotion that you felt when you experienced it and your listeners will feel the same warmth.

Good conversations are not soon forgotten. They are informative. They are inspiring. They motivate. They make life a little better and a bit more thrilling. They pack Power.

23

THE POWER WAY TO HANDLE
QUESTIONS FROM THE AUDIENCE

"Mr. Speaker," said the chairman, "will you be willing to answer a few questions at the end of your speech?"

Will you, Mr. Speaker? I'll wager you five bucks to a plug nickel that your chin will fall on your chest and your eyes will bug out and your breath will come in hot pants—*unless you are a Power Speaker!*

I'm quite sure you're going to make a good speech tonight. You have prepared that speech well. You know exactly what you want to say. You've said it many times before. You've never had the least bit of trouble getting it said. *But you never had to answer questions when it was over!* What questions will they ask? What if you don't know the answers? What if you make a big fool of yourself?

WHENCE COMETH SUCH POWER

"I'll be glad to answer questions," says the Power Speaker.

Why will he be glad? Why is he not afraid to face the unknown? Whence cometh all this confidence? By now you surely know the answer: because he has developed the habit of *painting mental pictures;* because he dearly loves to paint these pictures; because nothing he has ever done with his brain has paid off so much; because he thinks in pictures and he speaks in pictures and he listens for pictures and he reads for pictures; because he has strung together from his Long Sheet a pattern of pictures supporting a theme and expounding a cause and forming a speech that he will now deliver to these people and then stand by for questions.

His confidence comes from knowing that he has used only 10 percent of the material he gathered on the Long Sheet in preparing his speech, from knowing that any question asked about his subject will call up from his feeling-brain a suitable picture with which to answer that question, from knowing that the only thing to fear from these questioners is fear itself because fear will stifle his feeling-brain and drive it slinking into the back alleys of his cranium and from knowing that a show of confidence as he faces any questioner will stimulate his feeling-brain into a picture-popping mood. All these things the Power Speaker knows. *Such knowledge gives him confidence. His cause gives him courage.*

TOSSING GLORY RIDERS OFF YOUR BACK

"I'll answer questions," says the Power Speaker, "but, Mr. Chairman, I'll throw the meeting right back into your lap before you can say Bodiddly Brown if a Glory Seeker rises up!"

In almost every audience of any size sits some lonesome soul who feels he must parade his poor person before the multitude or perish. As soon as the toastmaster announces that a question and-answer period will follow the speech, this ego-starved hombre will start cranking up his awareness so he can snatch a little attention and ride to glory on the back of the speaker. He will listen attentively to the speech until the speaker expresses an opinion that is debatable. All opinions at best are a leap ahead of the facts and many of them can be debated. So when the Glory Seeker finds a juicy plum among the speaker's opinions against which he can work up a good appetite, he jumps on it and plucks it and squeezes it with all of his glory-seeking mind and sits there during the remainder of the speaker's presentation formulating a little rebuttal to be used during the question-and-answer period to follow. He already knows the speaker's answer to the question he plans to ask. He figures to ask the question, await the answer, and then grab the limelight and put the speaker down hard with his rebuttal. Afterwards, he expects to go striding forth feeling in the depths of his bones that he is a heroic human being.

If you ever encounter one of these hungry egos, and you certainly may do it because they are there, take a tip from yours truly: just toss a friendly salute at the microphone and walk calmly to the toastmaster's chair.

"Mister Toastmaster," you will say, "I return the meeting to you—my presentation is concluded."

Thank goodness that most toastmasters are adept at handling Glory Seekers, and praise Allah that most audiences are great at hissing down such parasitic creatures—especially if you have done a great job with your speech.

"Back to the boondocks, obstreperous Glory Seeker! Hiss! Hiss! Hiss!"

WHETHER TO HOLD A QUESTION-AND-ANSWER PERIOD

You may not want a question-and-answer period at the end of your speech.

"Mr. Chairman," you explain, "when I wind up my speech and pop my proposal, you better jump out of the way because the walls of this room will come tumbling down as these people go forth to answer my call. Phone me later if there are questions."

On the other hand, if you are running for public office or stumping for a new jail or delivering any speech loaded with facts and figures that could be misinterpreted, you may even take the initiative and suggest to the chairman that you will be happy to answer questions at the end of your presentation.

ONE VITAL PRECAUTION

If you do hold a question-and-answer session, one thing is absolutely vital: be sure you *repeat the question* over the microphone to the entire assembly the moment it is asked. A question from out of the heart of a big audience may not reach the ears of those sitting apart from the questioner. Anybody who fails to hear the question will start gathering wool. A lot of wool gathering can choke out much of the good you have done with your fine speech and your meeting can fall flat on its face. Repeating the question so all can hear puts everybody in the room on the team, so that each person stays alive and vibrant and pays attention to your answers.

LITTLE PAUSES THAT REAP REWARDS

Actually a question-and-answer period can be the highlight of your performance. As the question comes floating up from the audience, a picture or two with which to reply will come popping into your mind. Then, as you repeat the query for the benefit of the audience, a few more pictures will come so that you will be well-fortified with answers. You may not feel as free and easy as you did delivering your prepared address, but the little pauses in your speech as you search for the best answers and the little glances that you cast off into the wild, blue yonder as you grab for facts and figures will draw you closer to your listeners because they will get the idea that these little hesitations mean you are really in there giving these questions your best thought—you are working hard for this audience and they like you for it.

THREE LITTLE WORDS THAT PACK AWESOME POWER

Suppose a tough question comes and no picture pops. You are stuck in the mud with nothing to unload. Not so, Mr. Speaker, because you have an answer to that question and it is the only right answer and that answer is one of the most powerful replies known to man:

"I don't know!"

Oh what power vibrates in that simple little sentence! *You don't know!* Do you realize what that answer tells me, Mr. Speaker? Your admission that *you don't know* stands up and shouts in my face that you *did know* what you were talking about in that fine speech of yours and that everything you said was the gospel truth. Anyway I am willing to bet on you and vote for you and fight for you. How refreshing to meet a man who admits he doesn't know.

"I don't know but I'll find out and I'll call you."

That's the way the Power Speaker handles questions from the audience.

So, Mr. Speaker, unless you want immediate action on your proposal the moment you pop it, don't hesitate to hold a question-and-answer period right after you have poured out your heart and your mind to your people. The extra session can be exciting and it may get you elected to office or get the jail built or get a few misunderstandings straightened out.

Any questions?

24

MAGNETIC EYE OF THE POWER PLANT

"Congratulations, Joe! You won the trip to Hawaii!"

The boss meant that Joe with his entire family—lovely wife, fine youngsters, and himself—would fly first class, all expenses paid, into the heart of the blue Pacific and lounge on beautiful sand beaches and roam exotic landscapes and sleep and eat in ocean-splashed hotels for two solid weeks.

Nice going, Joe. What Joe did to earn all this was sell more dog food than any other salesman in his company. And Joe was only a few years out of college, where I had given him a grade of C in public speaking! C is an average grade. Joe came to our university with an average high school record, performed on our campus in an average way, and graduated with an average college record (except it took him four years to pass two years of Spanish).

But Mr. Joe Average-in-All-Things had way down deep in his internal workings a lurking tiger that put Power into everything he said: *he had a sparkle in his eyes when he talked.*

AVERAGE SPEAKER WITH A SPARKLING FUTURE

We grade a speaker on his preparation and his delivery, on what he says and how he says it. That's all. Joe always—I mean absolutely *always*—came poorly prepared to the platform. I don't suppose he worried about a single thing in all this world. When he started to talk we thought we had his theme right away because he always turned us on with a sharp word picture; but his theme invariably turned out to be something else and most times we were not sure it was even that. Fuzzy in theme, wobbly in support, and weak in proposal, Joe gave an average performance in public speaking class. For preparation I would have graded him zilch except that he did paint pictures with his words, although you hardly knew what theme he was sounding in his introduction or supporting in the body of his speech or echoing in his conclusion. Sound! Support! Echo! Absolute non-expendables in Power Speaking. *But* there were good word-pictures throughout Joe's entire presentation, and plenty of them.

Joe stood up there on the platform looking like the average mortal he was and sounding like the average speaker who came day in and day out to our speech classes—*except for the sparkle in his eyes when he talked.* However I had to give Mr. Joe Average a pretty good grade for his delivery. Do you know why? He had the attention of his audience; he made a listener out of every person in the room. Audiences kept looking and listening and waiting for his message to come through and they were still waiting when he sat down and when he did sit down they looked at Joe with sagging jaw and open mouth.

"What do you propose, Man?" they seemed eager to ask

Even though Joe delivered a fuzzy message, he made people look when he started to speak and he kept them listening as he talked and he had them interested *in him as a person* when he sat down, although they hardly knew what he had proposed.

> "Did you hear Joe's speech?"
> "Yes."
> "Did you like it?"
> "Yes."
> "What did he talk about?"
> "I don't know, he didn't say."

Yet a couple of years later Mr. Joe Average-in-All-Things flew his whole "famn damily" first class to Hawaii for two weeks and it didn't cost him one red cent, all because Joe was the best darn salesman in his company.

MAKING THE EYES PERFORM LIKE MAGNETS

I'll tell you the gospel truth, my reading friend: I knew for sure when Joe Average left college he would turn out to be a super salesman because *he had a sparkle in his eyes when he talked!*

Do you know what a sparkle in a speaker's eye does to a listener? It draws him like a magnet. Here's what it did for Joe:

> "I like you," said that sparkle.

Joe's liking you made you feel better and feeling better you enjoyed life a little more. You began to like Joe. "Joe likes me. I like Joe. We are one in spirit. We *identify*. May we survive together." You wanted Joe to survive as a speaker. So you gave him what every speaker needs to survive, your attention. And I gave him C in the speech course because he failed to give me a specific message.

"I give you *recognition*," said the sparkle in Joe's eyes, even though Joe the first time he mounted the platform was looking at these classmates for the first time in his life. In suggesting *recognition* with his eyes Joe was feeding the second greatest hunger that gnaws at the innards of all mortal beings. "Joe gives me recognition. I give Joe recognition. We are one in spirit. We *identify*." So you sit listening for Joe's message and I get ready to flunk him on preparation unless some message starts coming through.

"You thrill me," says the sparkle in Joe's eyes. Thrills come from romance and romance is the third greatest hunger that burns in the human torso. Romance is not necessarily sexual; any thrilling experience is romantic. "I thrill Joe. Joe thrills me. We are one in spirit. We *identify*. Long live both of us!" So you hang in there patiently waiting for Joe to get his message across—me too.

The message never comes. Joe's preparation is bad. But when he sits down you sit looking at him with interest *sparkling in your eyes*. You *identify*. And I give him C in the public-speaking course—bad preparation plus good delivery equals average grade.

A SALES PITCH THAT CAN'T BE BEAT

Joe graduated and went to work for the Pacific Dog Food Company in San Jose, California. This year his company named him Salesman of the Year. Have fun in Hawaii, Mr. Super Salesman.

Not long after graduation, Salesman Joe came cadillacking back to the university one bright day and showed up in my office sporting a two hundred dollar suit of clothes and a fifty dollar pair of shoes and a fancy sample case that would have cost me a week's pay. He talked about his new job, selling dog food. He talked about his beautiful wife and his two fine youngsters. He talked about his brand new split-level home with its big mortgage and his new avocado-colored automobile with its big mortgage. *He spoke with a sparkle in his eyes.*

"I want to be the best goldarned dog food salesman in this country," he said.

"Joe, how good is your dog food?"

"Man, it's the best in the west. We put vitamins X, Y, Z, and Canine P in our dog food."

"Do the dogs like it?"

"They love it. Vitamin X makes our dog food look good, Vitamin Y makes it smell good, and Vitamin Z makes it taste good."

"But is it good for the dog?"

"Nothing better. Canine P puts vim, vigor, and long life into the body and thoughts of loyalty into the mind and feelings of tenderness into the soul of every dog that feeds on our food."

"Joe," I said, "you are a super salesman. You are selling a product that you make yourself believe in with all your heart and with all your soul. Your sales pitch is organized. In your introduction your theme is easy to understand and congenial to hear: 'Lady, I come to you bearing a precious package for your precious pet.' In the body of your sales talk you support your theme with vivid pictures easy to see and good to feel: 'X, Y, Z, and Canine P does etcetera and etcetera for your dog.' Then in your conclusion your proposal comes popping through as a natural consequence of what you have said: 'Our dog food makes life better and more thrilling for your dog and for you too because you *identify* with your dog, so buy my dog food today.' *And you speak with a sparkle in your eyes.* Incidentally, Joe, how about sending me a hundred boxes of dog food—I have two dogs and I identify with both of them."

When Joe Super Salesman comes cruising down your street in his high-priced automobile, when he comes knocking on your door in his high-priced clothes, when he comes flashing his high-priced brief case with its samples of Vitamins X, Y, Z, and Canine P, he will probably start the conversation by saying:

"How do, friend. I want to shake hands with your dog.
I want to *identify* with him. I come bearing a precious package
for your precious animal."

And he will speak with a sparkle in his eyes. That sparkle will hold you from turning him from your threshold. And he will sell you dog food.

THE SURE-FIRE WAY TO A CLIENT'S HEART

Mr. Power Speaker, you yourself may be the world's greatest potential salesman, but if you don't make yourself believe that the product you are selling is the best of its kind, so good that *your eyes sparkle when you speak of it,* you had better start believing and *sparkling* or get yourself a new product or ship off to the Isle of Sad Salesmen. That sparkle in your eyes leads your listeners straight to your heart where they find themselves liking you, wanting you to survive, wanting you to be recognized, and wanting life to be thrilling for you because they have identified with you, and a better, more thrilling life for you makes life better and more thrilling for them. A sparkling eye is a magnetic eye that comes reaching up out of the depths of your Power plant and draws dollars to your family bank account.

THE GLEAM AND GLINT THAT SAPS YOUR POWER

But, beware! If instead of giving a sparkling pitch for your product, you should happen to go booming down the road taken by the average salesman and start spieling off a venomous denunciation of some rival product that your customer has just mentioned, the sparkle in your eyes will turn into a snake-like gleam that will put your client on edge and prevent him from identifying with you. The sparkle becomes a gleam that comes across like a glare.

I want you to meet Big Sam Boston, who just recently shipped out for the Isle of Sad Salesmen. Big Sam came to college during the same year as Joe Average, and Sam was anything but average. He came packing two hundred forty pounds of physical power on his six-foot-four frame. As a sophomore he made the all-conference team as fullback. As a junior he displayed strong vote-getting power when he was elected president of his class. As a senior he showed great power in his thinking each day in speech class because he always came well-prepared. There was also power in the spirit with which he strode to the speaker's stand, pounded the podium for attention, and boomed forth his speech in a fog-horn voice. You had to give Sam Boston A for preparation and A for delivery because he put it all together before he came to class and he let it all hang out while he was up there performing. The man had tremendous power, no question.

Now hear this: I knew for certain when Big Sam Boston left college that he would never win any free trips to Hawaii for his salesmanship. Here's why: *He had a gleam in his eyes when he talked that turned into a snake-like glint when he was challenged.*

When Big Sam addressed an audience, you looked and you listened. You were afraid not to. You expected any moment Big Sam, if he happened to catch you gathering wool, would come charging down upon you from the platform and lower the boom on your mid-region and knock you into the middle of next week. You had to be forever ready to duck when he came. So you looked and listened.

Then one dark day you approached Big Sam after class

and pulled the dumbo act of the year: You challenged Old Super
Muscle on some statement he had made in his speech and the
gleam in Sam's eyes became a glint that threatened to pierce
your eyeballs and scorch the color from each retina. You crossed
him no more, did you, my friend?

KILLING A SALE WITH A LOOK

Sam graduated way above average and went to work selling
automobiles for a top-notch agency in Cincinnati, Ohio. He sold
a good automobile, one of America's finest. But he barely made
a living selling a great product. Why? There is only one reason:
*He had a gleam in his eyes when he talked that became a snake-like
glint when he was challenged.*

"I hate . . . ," says that snake-like glint. Anybody who
hates looks hateful, and that ever-present watchdog of the feeling-
brain known as the Power of Suggestion brings a host of icicles
clattering down upon those who stand witness. Says Sam's customer to himself, "This salesman doesn't like me. I don't like
him either. We are divided in spirit. We *fail to identify.* I want
him to go away." And Sam's prospect grabs the doorknob firmly
in his right hand.

"I refuse to recognize . . . ," says that snake-like glint
in Sam's eyes, and his customer flexes the muscles in the arm
holding the doorknob.

"You depress me . . . ," says that snake-like glint, and
Sam's man then performs a courageous act: He puts the flat
of his foot on the seat of Sam's britches and the fight of the
century is now underway. It is a modern David against Goliath
contest and, as always, David comes out the winner because
Big Sam loses the sale and ships sorrowfully off for the Isle
of Sad Salesmen.

You just waltz yourself up to the betting booth and plop

down your bottom dollar that any strong denunciation of a rival product in front of a prospective customer will stamp a menacing look on your face that will send the prospect into a defensive stance and kill all chances of your making a sale.

THE POWER WAY TO SELL YOUR GOODS

Today Joe Average is a super salesman because Joe possesses Power that is magnified by the sparkle in his eyes when he talks. Sam Boston is a poor salesman because his power is *sadly diminished* by the gleam in his eyes when he talks and *absolutely nullified* by the snake-like glint when he's challenged.

Mr. Power Salesman, let's wrap it up with one simple proposal: Fill yourself so full of enthusiasm for what you are selling that it bubbles out through your eyes, lay off your competitors, and sell dog food.

This is Power Salesmanship.

25

GENERATING POWER
WITH A GAVEL AND A VOICE

"We must consult living men," said Cardinal Newman,
"and listen to living voices."

Remember a few chapters ago when you attended a company
conference at your steel mill? And remember what a good job
you did that day, how you impressed those company big-shots
with your Conference Comments? So fine a job in fact that the
Boss called you in a short while later for a two-man conference
which ended with an executive order:

"Call together all labor foremen and discuss the following
question: What can we do to raise our wages without raising
our prices?"

THE HEART AND SOUL OF A CONFERENCE

Well, Mister Speaker, you will soon come face to face with a new experience: attending a conference where you will be the leader, the take-charge guy, the guiding light. You can handle it too, because having reached these pages you have already become a Power Speaker. However, there are a few things about conferences you and I did not discuss before. Let's talk about them now. First a bit of background:

Any time two or more people sit down together to work out a solution to a mutual problem, they are holding a conference. America is governed by conferences. Everywhere we look we see committees meeting and small groups discussing and large gatherings swapping ideas—in the business world, in politics, in academic circles, in professional organizations, in service clubs, and in every phase of American public life.

The American system is a way of managing public business by public discussion that starts with a leader and stops with a leader. Many countries don't use public discussion; they use propaganda. But discussion puts the spirit of science into places where science can't go: ethics, judgments, and conscience. The greatest problem ever put to any discussion group is the question put to a jury: "Is this man guilty or not guilty?" No substitute exists for judgment in human affairs. And the most important event in all of history was the birth of conscience in man. Ethics, judgments, and conscience—these three qualities—are the heart and soul of a conference.

LIVING MEN WITH LIVING VOICES

"America is a talking government," said Benito Mussolini, and he was right. He didn't mean to be complimentary, far from it, but he was—most complimentary. What he meant was that

the American way of solving a problem was to appoint a committee or call together a discussion group or announce a public
meeting, all of which he thought would take too much time
to get anything done.

Fascist Italy handled its problems by executive order. So
did Nazi Germany. So do Communist Russia and Red China.
But the slow-moving democratic American system consults living
men grouped about conference tables and listens to living voices
and sweats out laborious conclusions, the whole operation con-
trolled by ethics and judgments and conscience.

No society anywhere on earth, past or present, has accepted
discussion more widely and more freely as a part of the life
of all the people as has this Land of the Pilgrims Pride. And
what has it gotten us? This, *this*, THIS: Freedom to talk things
over has accounted for the tremendous production capacity of
the American people to rise up in time of stress and successfully
meet the attack of other nations who were supposed to be better
prepared for quick action and successful results with their do-
it-now executive decrees than were we with our cuss-
and-discuss-what-the-hell-should-we-do conferences.

We have our executive orders. We have our take-charge
guys, our whip crackers. When we want the trains to keep running
on schedule, or wages and prices to stay put for awhile, or an
atomic bomb to drop, somebody orders it done. However it takes
a lot of consulting with living men and a lot of listening to
living voices around a lot of conference tables to make better
railroads and stronger economy and nobler relationships with
foreign folks.

HOW TO HANDLE TALK THAT GOES NOWHERE

So the Boss said to you, "Call together all labor foremen
and discuss the following question: What can we do to raise
our wages without raising our prices?"

Not that I want to put you under pressure, friend, but did you know that the success of this conference will depend on the leader? Let me have a little harmless fun with you by poking a few basic questions right between your eyes:

1. How will you open the conference?
2. How will you manage cross talk when two hog-balling members of your group refuse to give up the floor and the air goes bad with static?
3. What will you do when a couple ornery pilgrims start hurling verbal abuse at each other?
4. How will you get the discussion off dead center when there comes a lot of talk-talk-talk but little point-point-point?
5. What will you do about the intelligent shy-guy in the meeting—and there will be quite a few who will sit in stony silence.
6. How will you deal with the hard-heads who come to the conference with their minds already made up on the issues at stake?
7. How will you close the conference?

COMING PREPARED WITH POWER TURNED ON

I entertain no doubts about your forthcoming success in this venture. As a Power Speaker you will come prepared to the conference hall. You will lay an outline on the table before you, a work-sheet to be used as a guideline to keep the discussion on point. You will make a few introductory remarks:

"Gentlemen, we come to discuss a vital issue. We do not start with a proposition. We start with a question. We seek an answer.

"In this meeting I want everybody here to stand up and say what he feels and thinks. And I want all of us to sit and listen to what everybody else has to say. But I want us all to keep in mind that we are looking for the best answer to a vital question: What can we do to raise our wages without raising our prices?''

Then you throw the meeting open for comments, and the discussion starts; your conference is under way. As the leader you have the authority to speak up any time you wish, but you will not sit up there with your big gavel in your hand looking like God's gift to lesser folks. Your job is to stimulate, to ask challenging questions, to keep the discussion moving head-on toward the problem.

Somewhere early in the proceedings you will want to issue a helpful warning:

"Gentlemen, don't jump to conclusions. Get a lot of for-instances before you generalize."

A brother of mine is a school board lawyer in one of the large school systems in southern Ohio. He wrote me recently about a meeting of his board in which one of the newly elected members, who evidently wanted to show the older heads about the table that he intended to be a Power-packed plugger for the people, made the following speech:

"Too many of our teachers live outside our school system. Our people pay taxes to pay our teachers and our teachers spend that money elsewhere. That ain't right."

"Bill," said the superintendent, "do you know how many actually live outside?"

"Not exactly," said Bill, "but Francis White does and so does Harvey Johnson."

A check of the school roster showed that of 2039 employees of the school board only nine lived outside the city limits and seven of those on small farms that were included within the school system.

Get a lot of for-instances before you generalize.

As your conference rolls along you may wish to point out issues that have not been touched. Through it all you will guide but you will not dictate.

"Just what is your point, Tony?" you will say if Tony gets carried away with his own cuteness and strays far from the subject.

You will equalize the participation when Elmer, the company rabble-rouser, grabs the spot light and holds forth long and loud with no apparent intention ever to stop.

"I think we have your point of view, Elmer. Now let's hear from the others. We'll come back to you."

RAPPING WITH A SOOTHING TOUCH

You will keep the peace. When tension begins to arise you will seem to ignore it at first as you spin off a funny story in the manner of Abraham Lincoln when his cabinet sessions threatened to get stormy. You can use light-hearted words, spoken in a sincere manner, to make a serious point to the others: *Shut up.*

Or you may at times rap gently with your gavel and, still trying to stay out of the fight, make a pretty little speech:

"Gentlemen, we are all of us full of fine spirit and definite ideas and that's wonderful, but we've got to remember that the greatest sin in a conference is for somebody to get mad."

If the ruffled spirits continue to harangue and harass and storm clouds begin to form over your conference room, you will have to point your finger and take a definite stand:

"Jerry! You have said enough! You too, Clarence! I want

you fellows to cool off! Meanwhile the rest of us will talk
a bit. We'll come back to you men later.''

Sometimes a resounding "Shut up!" becomes necessary.
After your conference has had a fair chance to express itself
and then suddenly all hell seems ready to break loose in spite
of your gallant efforts to stem the tide, you will just have to
take a firm grip on your gavel and give the table a whole series
of resounding smacks and put a little lightning in your eye and
a bit of thunder in your voice and issue an executive order:

> *"This conference is adjourned!* Next meeting will be next
> week same place same time and I will appoint some big-muscled
> stewards to help me keep order. Good night.''

CLOSING YOUR CONFERENCE THE WINNING WAY

You have tried to be gentle but at the same time you have
been firm. You have been congenial but still you have been
pretty tough. You have been patient but you have been decisive.
And through it all you have been fair to everybody present,
and all of them will go away respecting you for your ability
to lead a conference. If somebody approaches you later with
the declaration that you adjourned the meeting without a motion
and a vote, you simply inform that wise acre that in times of
stress a leader must forget Roberts Rules of Order and act as
he sees fit. Every responsible soul in your organization will back
you to the hilt on your way of taking charge.

At your second session your question for discussion will
be: How well did we succeed at our last meeting? You will
then give a summary of the other meeting and start the discussion
anew. At the end of the session you and your conferees will
appraise all the data gathered, draw conclusions, and prepare
a report for the Boss.

A COON SKIN CAP AND A SMILING VOICE

Ben Franklin was one of America's most successful conferees. He did his greatest work at age 73 when he put on his
coon skin cap and sailed off for the peace conference in Paris
to help appraise the results of the American Revolution. He
departed these shores with the cries of his countrymen ringing
in his ears that he must not—absolutely must *not*—come home
with less land than that comprising the original thirteen colonies.
Franklin came home grinning like the cat that ate the canary,
waving land deeds to all territory in this country west to the
Mississippi River. For years afterward, young America came
and worshipped at the shrine of this great Power Conferee.

Ben Franklin's greatest strength? *He had a sparkle in his
eye and a smile in his voice when he talked.*

SUBTLE QUESTIONS THAT WIN YOU FRIENDS

"I never give orders," said a successful chairman of the
board of directors of one of America's greatest manufacturing
companies, "I just ask questions." Yet his people always gave
considerable thought to his point of view, and he reflected that
point of view in the way he asked his questions:

"Isn't it true that . . . ?"

"Don't you feel that . . . ?"

"Haven't you seen cases where . . . ?"

Questions like these are subtle. While they imply respect
for the opinions of the listeners, each question presents to each
listener a speaker confident he is right and confident that his
listeners will nod approval. This show of confidence by the
speaker works on the feelings of those who listen so that any
who may be undecided on the issues at stake find themselves

flashing a green light as the great Power of Suggestion draws them closer to the questioner. They *identify* with him.

Even those people who normally would have answered no to the question feel themselves restrained from shaking their heads in denial because such a question seems to ask the listener to make a decision, to be his own man, to think. He likes that. He likes to be considered a thinker. He likes the leader for asking the question. It was a compliment. Actually subtle questions cause listeners to feel something and the thing they feel makes them think and what they think tends to be what the questioner wanted them to think.

Subtle questioning can accomplish more than strong assertion if your conferees are opposed to the ideas you were about to assert before you decided to go subtle instead.

If you would like to grade yourself on your performance as leader of the conference just held, how well did you succeed in the following?

1. Explaining the problem.
2. Starting the discussion.
3. Eliciting responses.
4. Keeping friendly control.
5. Offering running commentaries.
6. Handling conflict.
7. Appraising the discussion.
8. Summarizing and concluding.

THE BRAINSTORM

Now let's have some fun. Suppose that instead of starting out with a formal conference to figure out ways and means of raising wages without raising prices, you decide first to throw a Brainstorm Session on the same subject and follow later with your regular conference. This can be very rewarding.

Our college public-speaking professor once invited a group

of eight professional cartoonists, all established artists, to come to our class and put on a Brainstorm Session. They came and sat at a round table on a stage in front of our class, behind them a big easel filled with a sheaf of large drawing paper. After our prof had introduced each cartoonist, whom incidentally he had snatched from their annual convention being held in our college town, their leader went to the easel and drew a picture of a tree. Nothing more. Just a simple tree.

"Now, my faithful compatriots of the cartoon art," said the leader, "somebody get up and add something to go with my little tree. Whatever pops into your curly head. Don't try to think. I don't want you to think. I want you to feel. Loosen up. Relax. Suppress your conscious mind. Allow your subconscious to take over. Let the spirit move. This will be creative art at work. Hop to it, men. Who's first?"

One by one, again and again, to and fro, for one solid hour these fine professional artists leaped to the easel, filled page after page with cartoon after cartoon, some funny, some serious, some simple, some complex, but all so spontaneous and excellent and entertaining that the meeting was one of the most exciting hours I have ever known in a college class room. We were witness that day to a Brainstorm Session at work in living color.

QUICK-FINGER WORK AND RAPID-FIRE TALK

So you call your people together, give them the problem to be solved, and start a Brainstorm Session. I hope you brought a tape recorder with you or else one of those quick-fingered señoritas with one of those rapid-fire machines that can knock out a couple hundred words per minutes. Otherwise, your ordinary secretary with a run-of-the-mill typewriter may go stark, raving mad trying to keep up with the business that will go bounding about this conference hall today.

"How can we solve this problem, gentlemen? Talk to me,

everyone of you, but one at a time . . . hold your hands up . . . snap your fingers if you want priority . . . let there be never a dull moment . . . down with restraint . . . speak up the instant something pops . . . don't try to think . . . just talk . . . don't ask yourself whether it will sound silly . . . out with it . . . get rid of all self-doubt . . . let spontaneity flow . . . to hell with analysis and criticism . . . we'll evaluate later . . . quantity counts, not quality . . . maybe there will be only one good suggestion out of a hundred . . . so let's get in a thousand suggestions . . . who wants to talk first?"

From that moment on you will do very little leading, just directing traffic. If there is a lull in the verbal flow you will want to shoot provocative questions to your people to keep things moving:

"Where would we get it?"

"How much would it cost?"

"How many people would it take?"

Your questions must never reflect a critical attitude nor should you permit any member to criticize or deride any other member. At any instance of criticism you should pound the gavel.

"Evaluation comes later!" you thunder, but there is a smile in your roar.

Even though you have asked each participant to raise his hand before speaking, you will have to allow this rule to be flexible. Otherwise spur-of-the-moment comments would never come out because when chain reaction sets in, ideas come popping by the dozens and refuse to wait for pomp and ceremony.

CREATIVE THOUGHT IN ITS FINEST HOUR

How long should a Brainstorm Session last? It depends. It could be ten minutes. It could be an hour. It's up to you as leader to decide when to close. Caution: Sometimes the Brainstorm produces its best ideas in the late stages after the chain reaction has been going well, when off-the-top-of-the-head suggestions have given way to deeper ones, when the group has grown weary and the thinking-brain dull, while the feeling-brain still surges on forever active and unimpeded now by the conscious mind, when real creative art comes into its finest moments.

The Brainstorm is not everybody's cup of tea. It may appall the orderly and anger the precise, some of those engineering geniuses and mathematical whizzes and assorted fuddy-duddys who preach total efficiency for man and machine. However, the experience of many of our better American companies has shown the Brainstorm to be a most productive tool for chipping out ideas to form the agenda for a later conference. On with the Brainstorm!

If the time ever comes when we no longer have leaders capable of stepping forward and picking up a gavel and calling a conference to order to work out solutions to public problems, and if the time ever comes when we no longer have sufficient conferees who are willing to come to order, then this free-wheeling democratic system of ours will have to go take a rest while we call in a gang of two-fisted sluggers who will knock a few heads together until we get things straightened out again.

One big cheer for the American style conference and three big cheers to the man who can generate enough Power to lead one.

You can do it!

26

PUTTING POWER
INTO THE WRITTEN WORD

So you are determined to *read* your speech at the radio station? Okay if you insist. I can hardly blame you. Most people read radio speeches. There's just one thing I want to say and I want to say it with my fingers clutching your coat lapels with lightning in my eye and thunder in my baritone: *Read that speech the way you would speak it if you were not reading—make it sound like natural talk.*

HOW PEOPLE COME SNAPPING TO ATTENTION

If those people listening out there on the ether waves far beyond your radio mike get the idea you are reading to them, somebody will twist the dial and turn to a program more exciting. All of us speak many more words than we write and hear many more than we read. Most people don't like to write. Some don't even like to read. Very few want to be read to. The best way to put a lively youngster to sleep in his trundle bed at night is to read him a story—no better way. But everybody snaps to attention when he starts hearing you pour forth from the depths of your heart.

If we want to communicate with somebody miles away, we will grab a telephone and pay five bucks for a long-distance call, when all in God's world we would have to do would be to write a few words on a sheet of paper and lick a postage stamp and give and get the same information much more cheaply and in a more durable form.

Other times we'll stop the car and ask a policeman the way to a place instead of reading the map on the seat beside us. When we register for a convention, we'll pick up a set of instructions on how to register, give the thing a limpid look, and then drop it.

"How do I register?" we say to the man at the registration desk. If he picks up the sheet of instructions and starts to read to us, we'll put a tender hand on his shoulder.

"Don't read to me, mister. I can read for myself. Just talk to me in a friendly voice. I'm a long way from home. I'm lonely."

We would rather talk than write. We would rather listen than read. But we want people to talk *to* us, not read *at* us.

So if you insist on reading your speech into that microphone, you've got to fool that unseen listener and *read the way you speak when you're not reading.* It will take a little doing—I mean quite a bit of doing—to read with Power. It can be done. Most people don't do it. You can.

LOOKING AT WORDS BUT SEEING IDEAS

Remember during those times when you were standing before an audience delivering a Power Speech from a podium how you saw an orderly array of vivid pictures flowing across your mental screen? Remember how words to describe those pictures came popping into your mouth from God knows where? Remember how delivering a Power Speech the Power Way was one of the easiest things you ever did in your life?

Well, Power Speaking and Power Reading are two different breeds of cat, although they sound the same—almost. Since you are a Power Speaker you certainly can become a Power Reader. One big problem needs to be solved: How are you going to push those written words away from your conscious mind so you will sound like a speaker and not a reader?

Just suppose that instead of reading your speech you decided to memorize it word for word and recite it into the microphone. Had you done this you would have faced the mike and started to speak with nothing but fuzzy little words crossing your mental viewgraph. You memorized words. Now you have to recall words. You just might blank out the way young Winston Churchill did the first time he faced Parliament with a memorized speech. You could flounder and flop. At best your radio audience would hear a speech that sounded like somebody reading an essay. People don't like to be read to. They want to be "spoke" to. So here's a definite no-no: *Don't memorize that speech.* If you write it out, then read it, but put it over with Power. It's really not all that difficult.

Here you sit before a radio mike, your manuscript before you, bravely trying to read as though you were speaking, trying to send your message out into listening-land like a Power Speech. Something gets in your way. Know what? Words, written words. There is only one way to get those pesky little critters out of your conscious mind. Brand the following formula on your brain; drive it into your heart:

1. Give those written words *a relaxed stare* and see them as *groups of ideas.*
2. With your mind's eye *see the pictures* the written words

are describing—all those lovely little scenes you arranged in such orderly fashion when you were building your speech.

3. *Feel the emotion* aroused by those moving mental pictures.

4. *Speak* those written ideas the way you *feel* those tumbling pictures.

5. Read your speech *the way you would say it if you were not reading.*

6. That's Power Reading—there is no other way to put Power into the written word.

OH HOW LONELY IS A RADIO ROOM

The studio will be a lonely place, deathly quiet. Nowhere about you is there a sparkling human eye you can gaze into and feel the *esprit de corps* of give and take: "I give you my speech, you give me your attention—we're tuned in."

Warning: Don't let the funeral parlor stillness lull your voice into a dreary monotone. Keep watching those exciting pictures flowing by on your mental screen, keep giving your manuscript a relaxed stare, and keep feeling what you're saying—keep reading with Power.

Here's another little tip to help you ward off a lethargic voice: Summon up the bright-eyed image of a distant friend or loved one sitting home in his living room beside his radio or out on the road in his automobile or down town at his favorite bar, and pour your message into his eager ears. Read your speech to that far-away friend so that he will think you are speaking from the heart, and not reading from a manuscript.

LIKE AN AWNING FLAPPING IN AN ANGRY WIND

Try this idea: Use triple space when you type your manuscript so that there will be lots of blank paper around the words making them easy to see. Remember that you have to use a relaxed stare as you read. You sure can't relax your stare if you have to squint to see. Also it's not a bad idea to use soft paper that won't crackle and pop as you lay one sheet aside and pick up another. Regular paper is so noisy that the microphone will pick up the rustling and send it along like an awning flapping in an angry breeze or a bunch of disturbed workmen crushing wooden orange crates with their feet.

"Aha!" exclaims the unseen listener. "This guy's reading that goldarned speech!" You're going to read it all right, but he is not going to know it because you are going to read it the Power Way.

THE AWFUL SOUND OF SILENCE

There in the solitude of that lonely broadcasting studio with nobody watching, you will let your gestures flow freely so you can express yourself the way you feel. But watch out! Don't hit the microphone, don't pound the table, don't stamp your feet, or else your listeners will think somebody suddenly got you with a Saturday Night Special. You can let yourself go as long as you don't hit anything but the air around you.

Be sure to number the pages of your manuscript. Soft paper is light in weight and if the ventilating fan suddenly lifts Page Three and floats it to the floor and you find yourself jumping from Page Two to Page Four, you don't want too many seconds to go by before you recover the errant sheet, or the awful sound of silence will shake your listeners. Even three seconds is an eternity to a radio audience.

Your voice is absolutely all a listener gets in a radio broadcast. Remember we live in an eye-minded environment. Eighty-five percent of all we know came to us through our eyes, only 10 percent through our ears. When I can see you as you talk, I catch the look in your eye, which helps me feel what you are saying, as do also your facial expressions and your gestures. There is also that far-away look as you pause for the right words to express best what you want to say next, and I know from watching you in your hesitation that you, as speaker, are hanging in there working diligently for me, as listener, so I keep looking at you and listening to you and *identifying* with you.

But in a radio broadcast all I get from you are your words, and should you pause a second too long I think my radio has gone on the blink. I may even smack the blame thing with the heel of my hand to start it working again.

THREE LITTLE CHANGES IN A POWER-PACKED VOICE

There are three things about your voice that you need to vary in order to put Power into your words: pitch, volume, and tempo. Let's first take a dry run through all three:

To our psychology class one day came a hypnotist. He put the whole class to sleep en masse. He held a shiny silver coin in one hand and told us to fasten our gaze upon it.

"Take a deep breath," he said, "and hold it until I tell you to let it go. Suck it in deep, de-e-eper, de-e-e-eper. Hold it, ho-o-old it, ho-o-o-o-old it. Now close your eyes and slowly let it go, slowly, slo-o-owly, slo-o-o-o-owly."

He talked in a soft monotone.

"You feel good today," he murmured so-o-oftly, slo-o-owly. "You never felt so go-o-od in all your life. From the top of your head to the tips of your toes you feel so-o-o go-o-o-o-od."

The rest of it seemed like a dream until he snapped us out of it. What that man did that day was just the opposite of inspiration. He took all the starch out of our spines with his soo-oo-oothing monotone voice.

But you and I don't want to put people to sleep. We want to arouse them, to stiffen their backbones, to stick a ramrod along their spinal columns. We want to snap them upright in their chairs. We came not to hypnotize; we came to stir. We came to stimulate, to arouse, to inspire—even though we are reading our speech over the radio with nothing reaching our audience except our voices. However we cannot do the job unless we vary the pitch and the volume and the tempo.

A THING CALLED PITCH

In every word of more than one syllable we have to give one particular syllable top billing: We raise the first syllable in *Da*vid, the second in Go*li*ath, and the third in recog*ni*tion.

In every sentence of more than one word we have to raise one particular word higher than the others:

1. *I'll* not fight Goliath.
   (You can if you want to.)
2. I'll *not* fight Goliath.
   (You can't make me.)
3. I'll not *fight* Goliath.
   (I'll talk to him but not fight him.)
4. I'll not fight *Goliath*.
   (I'll fight any of his men but not him.)

In any paragraph of more than one thought, we have to emphasize one particular idea above the others:

With long strides George Washington reached the roughhewn table. He grabbed up the letter of resignation he had just addressed to the Continental Congress. He tore it in two—once, twice, three times—and hurled the pieces upon the floor. Then he threw himself into a chair at the roughhewn table and cupped his head in his hands and prayed to Almighty God to give him strength to stand up to the British and *regardless of what happened never under any condition to surrender.*

In any piece of writing comprising more than one paragraph, we must put the greatest emphasis on one particular paragraph near the beginning, the one that sounds the theme. This is the introduction to the subject. Then we come back strong near the end when we echo the theme and pop the proposal. This is the conclusion of the piece.

Thus we emphasize certain syllables to pronounce words, certain words to clarify sentences, and certain sentences to sound themes and pop proposals. Such is the importance of the thing called *pitch*.

A THING CALLED VOLUME

If we push more air through our vocal chords we will increase our volume and produce a louder sound. We add volume when we want to emphasize certain ideas. At other times we emphasize by easing up on the flow of air, dropping our voices almost to a whisper. Look at these examples:

Suppose you are strolling across a busy street some dark night deep in a brown study over the speech you are planning to read at the local radio station. Then, a truck driver comes screeching to a halt a few inches from your startled torso.

"Hey, there, fellow!" roars the booming voice of the two-fisted monster in the cab of the truck. You are shook.

Now suppose you are strolling along a quiet avenue smoking over that same speech on a balmy summer evening and from the darkness of an open window at your elbow comes the soft aspirate tones of a female:

"Hey, there, fellow."

Are you shook? You known darn well you are. Look at this one:

> One night a drunk decided to take a short cut home through a graveyard. A couple of grave diggers had just finished excavating an extra large hole for a man and wife who had been killed in an automobile accident and were to be buried side by side in this double grave the next day.
>
> The drunk fell into the grave. He leaped and scrambled and clawed, but he could not get out of the big hole. He yelled at the top of his voice trying to attract somebody's attention. Nobody heard him. Absolutely exhausted he sank down in the darkness and went to sleep in one corner.
>
> Sometime during the wee hours he was startled from his slumber by a blood-curdling shriek. Right there in front of his eyes was another poor soul who had fallen in. This fellow was also trying to leap and scramble and claw his way out, but it was no use. So the poor guy sank down exhausted in the darkness of an adjacent corner, unaware that he had a fellow sufferer.
>
> The drunk, fairly sober by now, sat unnoticed in his own dark corner, feeling that he ought to speak to his new companion. But how much volume should he use? If he came on too strong, the poor chap might conk out with heart failure. So he cupped his hands to his mouth and very softly whispered, "Hey there, fellow, you can't get out of here."
>
> *But he did!* Know why? He was *shook*.

We can emphasize parts of our speech sometimes by stepping up the volume and at other times by using soft tones. The secret is in the variation.

However, there is one place where a whisper is forever forbidden by the Noble Knights of Power Speaking. Great has been the multitude of Power-seeking pilgrims who have had their union cards yanked from their grasp and who have been turned out to pasture on the Isle of Powerless Speakers for violating the whisper rule. Sad, but true.

One such young man meant to say, "I always read my speeches with *Pow*er." What we heard him say was, "I always read my speeches with *Pow*—."

Another fellow tried to say, "I always paint vivid *pic*tures." What we heard was, "I always paint vivid *pic*—."

One pretty lass intended to say, "I always fill you with deep *feel*ing." What came to us was, "I always fill you with deep *feel*—."

Amazing is the number of would-be Power Speakers who permit their voices to drop dead at the end of a sentence when the last syllable is unaccented.

I like the way Glen Campbell sings a song. When he takes up his guitar and does "Galveston" he thrills me. The word Galveston is pronounced with the accent on the first syllable: *Gal*veston. In the song Campbell accents two syllables, the first and the last: *Gal*ves*ton*. The communication is great. The effect is thrilling. I like the way he sings.

But Glen Campbell is a poor reader of a prepared manuscript. Know why? His voice goes dead on the last syllable in a sentence *if that syllable is normally unaccented*. You can't even hear the syllable.

Recently Campbell read the commentary for a great TV show called *Flight of the Snow Goose*. The program was terrific—except for one thing: You could not hear the last syllable of at least half the sentences in the commentary. Glen Campbell, great singer though he be, will never be admitted into the Noble Knights of Power Speaking until he stops violating the whisper rule.

A THING CALLED TEMPO

Tempo is the other voice technique to vary as you read that radio speech. Tempo means the speed with which you pour out your words. When you are tying together a lot of fast action with long compound sentences, you ought to let your voice go travelling like a runaway train. Of if you are describing a picture with a lot of details and want your listeners to see the whole image all at once, you have to race through the scene at breakneck speed. For instance:

> "You can sit in your doorway with a 30-30 rifle in your hand while all the Chinese in the world, alive and coming alive, start strolling by in single file one yard apart, and you can commence picking them off one by one with your trusty thunderball as they pass; but no matter how long you sit there and blaze away, when you finally grow so old and feeble and weary that you can no longer pull a trigger, there will be more Chinese alive in the world than when you started. Theme: *If we can't beat 'em, let's join 'em!*"

If you wish to emphasize each detail in a scene, you will want to read your manuscript more deliberately and use shorter sentences:

> "How much will Lunar Bill 999 cost you and me? I'll tell you. Tie a string of ten-dollar bills to the roof of the Pentagon. Now stretch that beautiful string off into space. Tie the other end to the American flag that we stuck on the moon. See those beautiful ten-spots stretching forth in the sunshine? See them fluttering in the breeze? Two hundred forty thousand miles of the precious things. Whose money is it? You know darn well whose! It's your money! It's my money! It's our money! Call your congressman! Kill Lunar Bill 999!"

When you want your listener to absorb some of your "think stuff," you will need to slow down to a snail's pace:

There is a threshold that separates your conscious mind from your subconscious. You *think* with your conscious mind. You *feel* with your subconscious. Your subconscious has a built-in hot line that leads straight to the emotions. Only 10 percent of your total brain is conscious. Ninety percent is subconscious.

You have nine times as much power to *feel* as you have to *think*. Therefore your *feelings* are nine times as strong as your *thoughts. But thought plus feeling equals ten times the thought without the feeling!* Get it?

Pitch, volume, and tempo—these three—are the qualities of the human voice that you and I must vary to generate Power and hold a radio audience when we are reading our speech.

SUCKING SOUNDS AND STOP WATCHES AND PENCIL MARKS

Don't sit too closely to the microphone as you read, or every couple of sentences or so your audience will hear a sucking and a blowing sound. Maybe you don't have asthma but your listeners will give you credit for some kind of bronchial disorder.

If you are to speak on a fifteen minute program, there will be commercials at the beginning and end of your performance that will chop your air time down to not more than twelve minutes at the most. Check with the program director and find out exactly how much time you will have. You normally will read about 110 words per minutes, but when the adrenalin starts to squirt at broadcast time you may crank up your rate to 125. Get plenty of speech down on paper.

Practice with a stop watch and put a pencil mark at the end of each minute. On the next to last page put in a little extra stuff, illustrative material, that you can drop if you are running out of time. Keep the last page the way it is so you can read your conclusion and echo your theme and pop your proposal in all its glory.

WINDOW PEEPER WHO STOPS THE SHOW

Sitting there so all alone in that broadcast booth, you are cut off from the outside world except for one window. That window is very important. Keep your head facing in that direction during your recitation. The program director may be standing there flashing you signals. Remember that a radio station puts a premium on every single second. Look at what that program director is trying to convey to you:

1. Points his finger at you. (Begin your speech.)
2. Pushes his hands from his face. (Move further from the mike.)
3. Pulls his hands toward his face. (Get closer to the mike.)
4. Turns hands palms-up. (Speak louder.)
5. Turns palms down. (Speak more softly.)
6. Forms O with thumb and finger. (You're great, man!)
7. Makes quick circles with finger. (Speed up.)
8. Pulls hands slowly apart. (Slow down.)
9. Slashes throat vigorously with finger. (Stop! Time's up!)

THE RADIO VOICE THAT CHARMED A NATION

Radio made a great man out of Franklin Delano Roosevelt. Back in the early Thirties this new medium sent one of the greatest speaking voices of all time into millions of American homes. People all over this country sat upright in their living-room chairs soaking up FDR's "Fireside Chats," each listener feeling that the soothing sonorous voice was talking directly to him. The listener *identified* with the speaker. He wanted this Power Speaker to be his leader. So, with 80 percent of the newspapers coming out morning and evening in strong opposition, the great New Dealer's army of listeners marched to the voting places and sent Franklin Delano Roosevelt four times to the White House.

"He has a golden voice and a seductive radio technique," wrote one of his bitterest critics.

Said Roosevelt to Orson Welles, "You and I are the greatest actors in the country."

Whether you liked this man's political policies or not, don't bet against his being the foremost radio speaker our country has known.

THE CORNERSTONE OF COMMUNICATION

What FDR did with a radio, others can do today even more effectively with television. The medium is at hand. All we need do is put Power into our performance the way John Kennedy did in his duel for the Presidency with Richard Nixon in 1960.

"What began as a hobby has become the cornerstone of communication in our society," said Llewellyn White of the Federal Communications Commission.

Anyone today who achieves the least bit of prominence may be suddenly called in to face a television camera. It could be an interview. It could be a set speech.

The interview will be no particular problem for you. The person who interviews you will ask provocative questions about whatever made you prominent. All this will resemble the question-and-answer period at the end of a speech. You've done all this before. No sweat here.

The set speech will be old stuff too. You will prepare your material exactly as before. Your speech will be shorter. You can select the liveliest parts of any of your past speeches and you'll be in fine fettle. In setting you up for your TV speech, the studio engineer will transcribe your manuscript onto the teleprompter. Then he will proceed to roll your words before your eyes just as fast as you read. You will perform the way you did on radio, but man oh man the advantages you have now. People can see you, your facial expressions, your lip movements, your gestures. You're back on the platform once again where you have performed so well before.

Look out though, there are a few difficulties. You still cannot see your audience. They are scattered all about the country, in living rooms and bedrooms and bathrooms and hotel lounges and on bar stools, in singles and pairs and triples and assorted groups small and large. Once again you have to visualize your listeners as you did for radio. Forget the distractions, those ghostly figures drifting about the studio changing the light booms and setting the stage for the program to follow yours. These people don't seem the least bit interested in your fine speech. Don't let it shake you. Pay no attention to these ghosts. They are only earning their daily bread. See that little red light that jumps from camera to camera? That's the bouncing ball that leads to the hot camera. Following it will keep you looking straight into the eyes of your invisible audience making each of them feel that you are talking directly to him. And that's Power, man!

Those lights are pretty hot. Better not wear heavy clothes because beads of perspiration show up like shiny pearls in the eye of the TV camera. Also wear clothes with subdued colors because white reflects so much light that features become blurred and black absorbs so much that it glares.

". . . the cornerstone of communication . . ." the man said.

PULSATING POWER OF WRITTEN WORDS SPOKEN

I'll bet William Jennings Bryan is rolling in his grave as he watches what modern man is accomplishing with radio and television. No doubt the great silver-tongued orator of the turn of the century, if he were alive today, would turn on the Power of his voice and the Power of his personality and the

Power of his enthusiasm and Power Talk his way into the Presidency of this country.

Such is the tremendous force of the written word when spoken with Power.

27

DRAWING POWER
FROM A BODY BONE-WEARY

You may find yourself not wanting to believe this, but, scout's honor, it's the gospel truth: I taught school for thirty-six years, both high school and college, without missing a single day of work—6660 straight days with never a gold brick. I was entitled to ten days sick leave per year, ten days when I could have stayed home and loafed and drawn full pay. I retired with 360 such days available and unattended and down the drain Do you think I'm bragging? You bet your sweet life I am. I'm proud of that record, although I still keep my eyes peeled for the first human being who will grab my hand and say "Congratulations!" All I have ever received for my Spartan effort on the firing line has been a startled gasp that seems to say, "Oh, how stupid!" If I was stupid, I'm proud of my stupidity, just as proud as I am of the 78 percent won-lost record on the football field.

"Didn't you ever get up on school mornings with a headache?" you ask.

"Many times."

"Didn't you ever crawl out of the sack with a pain in your belly?"

"Many times."

"Didn't you ever struggle off to the school house with a little bug biting on your innards?"

"Many times."

"Then many times you went to school sick."

"Right."

"Oh, how stupid! Why did you do it?"

I did it because I found out early in my career as an English teacher and a football coach that when I stepped before a roomful of lively youngsters and looked into their eager eyes, mental pictures flashed and ideas popped and energy squirted and headaches vanished and belly pains disappeared and I never felt better in my life.

Sometimes I felt so good that I stuck a clinched fist in front of my chest and gave the class a power salute:

"Let's go! Let's fight! Let's win!" I taught Football-English—that's the best kind.

Mental pictures are Power. Man Power. Unlimited.

OH WHAT A DIFFERENCE A PICTURE MAKES

Florence Chadwick was the first woman ever to swim the cold twenty-one mile stretch of water between Catalina Island and the California coast. But she tried twice before she made it. The first time she swam for 15 hours and 55 minutes and then numb with cold reached frantically for the boat.

"Pull me up!" she cried. "I can't swim another stroke!"

"You've got it made!" shouted her helpers. "The shore's only *one mile away!*"

"Where?" she moaned.
"There!" they pointed.
"I can't see it! Pull me up! I'm drowning!"

She had swum twenty miles. She had only one mile to go. But she couldn't make it. Her energy was gone. The shore was right there in front of her. Her helpers could see it through the fog. She couldn't see it though. The fog was too thick and salt water speckled her goggles.

"Pull me up!"

Florence Chadwick had failed with the goal in reach because she could see nothing but fuzziness and bleakness. She could feel nothing but helplessness and despair.

"If only I could have seen the shore, I believe I could have made it," she said.

The next time she tried the stunt she swam through the same cold water to within a mile of the same shore and found the same kind of fog enveloping the shoreline and the same old devil sea splashing her goggles and she felt the same numbness wrecking her bones and the same tiredness paralyzing her muscles, but she swam on and made it.

"This time I saw the shore," she said.
"How could you see the shore? The fog was just as thick as before and the water was even rougher!"
"I saw it *in my mind*."

What a difference a mental picture makes! When your feeling-brain sees nothing but fuzziness and bleakness on the television screen of your mind, the poor thing collapses into one corner of its quarters and your power goes dead. But show that tempermental rascal a clear, vivid picture of the shore line ahead, the goal sought, and the blessed thing comes to life with a leap and a sizzle and slaps your adrenal glands into action and sends you such a surge of energy that you fight on and get your work done.

WITH SWITCH TURNED ON AND POWER BURNING

After a grueling practice on the football field one stormy afternoon, I crawled wearily into the Buick and spent three hours driving from Columbus, Ohio to Cleveland in a blinding snowstorm, a regular Buckeye Blizzard. When I finally arrived an hour late at the country club where I was to make a speech, the meal was over but speech time was at hand. I most certainly was in no condition to stand up and say I was happy to be there. I wasn't a bit happy. I was bone-weary and body-tired, also one seasick dog—and that's the worst kind.

Normally I don't get seasick. I can go boat rocking or auto wobbling or roller coaster plunging and feel nothing but exhilaration. Unless I am very tired. This time I was dog-tired. Whatever causes seasickness I found it that night like never before or since. Spinning head, nauseated stomach, wobbly knees, miserable life—I knew for sure I was going to die but I was afraid it wouldn't happen soon enough to get me out of that dog gone speech.

I made the speech. I did a pretty good job of it too. Know why? When I got up and looked the Cleveland Chamber of Commerce and their wives in the eye, these intrepid people who had braved this awful weather to attend their annual banquet and "hear that speaker from down at the Ohio State University," I saw pictures I wanted to paint with words on the minds of these fine people. My head stopped whirling. My mid-region ceased boiling. My knees quit crumbling. I made the speech and when it was over I was not the least bit ashamed to take the paycheck.

I discovered again that night what I had concluded so many times before: Calling up prepared pictures to our mental screen will cause words to flow into our mouths and energy to squirt into our muscles that will enable us, no matter how tired we are or how sick we feel, to do a good job on the podium and finish with a new zest for life. If a bug is gnawing away at our internal workings, a fresh flow of adrenalin just might snuff him out, or if the old ticker in our chest is pulsing its last feeble throbs, a squirt of adrenalin might be just the thing to prolong our days. One thing I know for sure: we have a beautiful chance to cross the Dark Valley of the Shadow with our switch turned on and our Power burning.

Mental pictures are Power. Man Power. Unlimited.

THE PART OF YOUR BODY THAT NEVER GETS TIRED

Thomas Edison actually didn't need a bed. He had one but he didn't sleep in it. He took cat naps on a table in his laboratory. If he went to all the trouble of putting on his pajamas and retiring for the evening the way normal people do, he wouldn't be asleep more than fifteen minutes until he would come leaping to the floor, bouncing into his laboratory, and experimenting with the brand new idea that had just come popping above the threshold during his short sleep. Edison very probably did not sleep a total of three hours a night.

You, the Power Speaker, generate your Power by arranging on your mental viewgraph a series of exciting pictures to make specific points in your speech. These pictures come up from below the level of your consciousness. They slide back when you are not using them. When you are tired or don't feel good your mind appears to be a perfect blank. Your head seems dead. You can't think. You don't want to talk. You want to rest. You're tired. You're sick.

I'll have to agree that you are in no condition to *make up* a new speech. But Mister Power Speaker, you are in one fine fettle to drag your feeble frame to the podium and deliver one of your old speeches *already prepared!* There is a part of your body that never sleeps, that never gets tired or sick, that is always at your beck and call every moment of every day your whole life through as long as a drop of blood flows or an ounce of energy burns or a spark of spirit prevails. You know very well by now exactly what it is: It's the tiger in your tank, your picture snapper, your idea popper, your word provider, your emotion arouser, your energy squirter, your God-given feeling-brain, *the real source of all human Power.*

Mental pictures are Power. Words are Power tools. Where Power is, words are also. Power to create. Power to destroy. Power to follow the leader ahead. Power to lead the follower behind. Word Power. Man Power. Unlimited.

Therefore, whether we are bone-weary or soul-sick or fresh as the morning dew, let's make a magnificent effort to get up and deliver that speech. We'll do okay. And we'll feel better when it's over. That's Power, Man!

28

MORE POWER TO YOU

"Give me what I cry for," moans Planet Earth as she goes spinning down toward the Twenty-first Century.

"I want a new Churchill," cries the thinking man.
"I want another Lincoln," cries the feeling man.
"I want a Bodiddly Brown," cries the man of action.

Truly what we all need above everything else is a small army of mothers and fathers and preachers and teachers and scout masters and athletic coaches and business men and professional persons, the likes of Churchill and Lincoln and Brown, whom the rest of us can *identify* with, have *confidence* in, and draw *courage* from, so that a goodly number of us will dedicate ourselves to the task of shoring the underpinnings of this unsteady House of Man.

Occasionally the lightning flashes and the thunder roars and

the heavens part and upon the scene strides that heroic human
animal known as the thinker-feeler-doer—the Churchill, the Lincoln, the Brown. He leaps to the podium and pounds his gavel
and calls the hodge-podge of milling humanity to order and leads
them to *think* his thoughts by making them *feel* his feelings and
then sends them soaring forth to *do* whatever he proposes. He
is a heroic fellow.

YOU CAN BE A HEROIC FELLOW

How sad that heroes are so few. Sad because any normal
human being can be heroic. *You* can be heroic. You have just
finished the course. The heroic person is the fighter against odds,
the David against Goliath, who comes up with a secret weapon
that gives him confidence and a cause that gives him courage.
His secret weapon is a *skill* he has worked on until he is good
at it and thrilled with it. His *cause* is a better, more thrilling
life for himself and for those with whom he identifies. Win,
lose, or break even, every human being is heroic who fights
a good fight.

> Said William Gladstone a hundred years ago:
> "*Power* is with the man who can *speak*."

THE LIVING POWER OF WORDS

Mental pictures are Power. Words are Power tools. Every
word I have written within these pages has been from me to
you. I give you something—my ideas, my thoughts, my feelings
—and you give me something—your attention. I have not
intended to transform you from something you were into something you were not. I have meant only to stir up the great potential
Power that lies deep within you, the greatest force available to
the service of man, the Power of Words. Man Power. Unlimited.

I have made proposals to you. What you do about them is your decision and yours alone. Nobody else can take credit. Your interests, your goals, your ambitions, will determine where you go from here. If you sally forth from these pages motivated to greater things, even though the words were mine, the decision was yours, the feeling and the thinking with which you greeted these ideas belong to nobody else but you; and the success you meet in the years ahead can be attributed solely to that enthusiastic reader who came with wide-open eyes and saw the Power Picture and felt the Power Feeling and used the Power Tools to exercise the Power Skill and do something about it all.

"Power is with the man who can speak."

Power Speaking is the *skill*, my faithful reading friend. A good, thrilling life is the *cause*. More Power and more Life to you and yours.

"Go get 'em, Tiger!"

INDEX